To: _____

From: _____

Date: _____

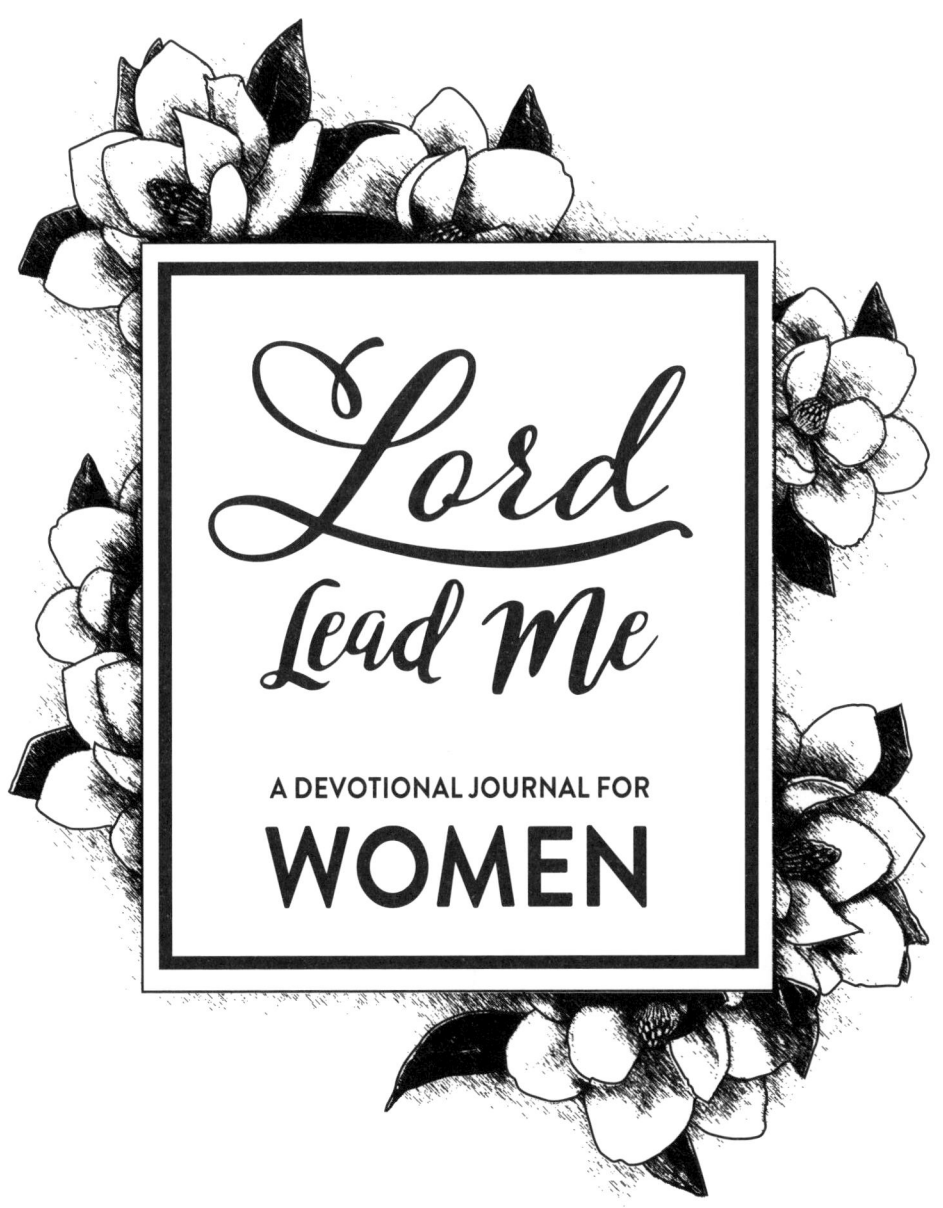

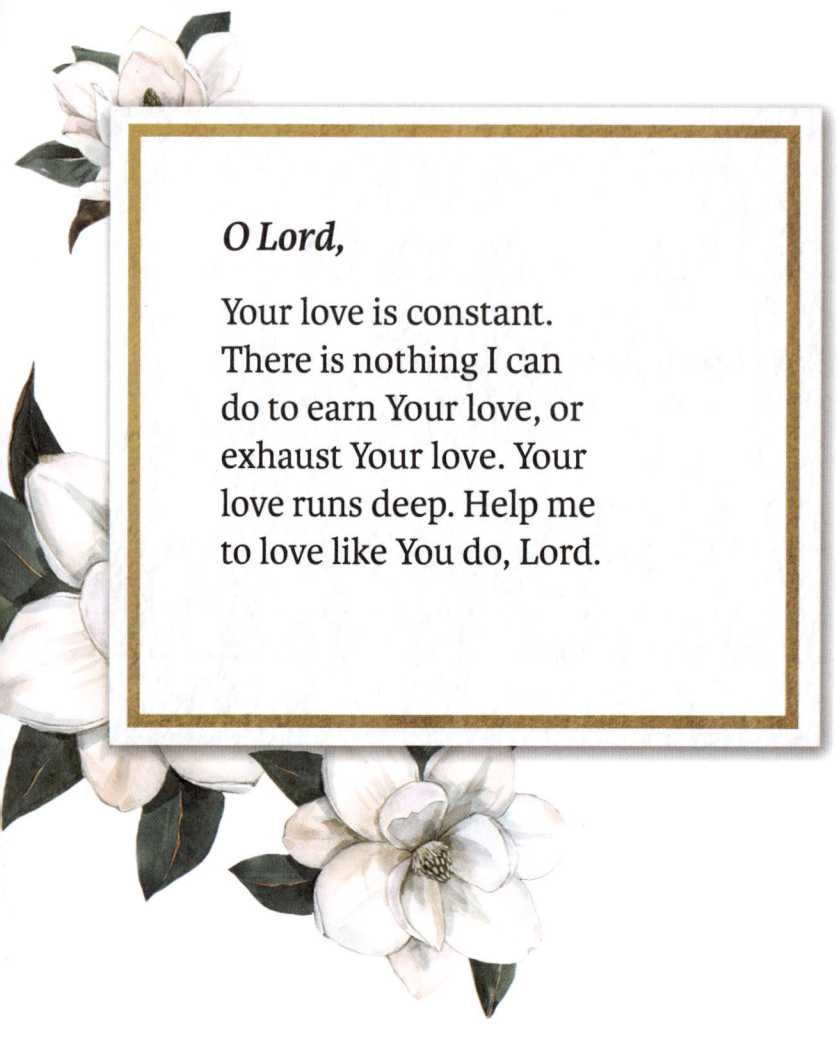

O Lord,

Your love is constant. There is nothing I can do to earn Your love, or exhaust Your love. Your love runs deep. Help me to love like You do, Lord.

The lovingkindnesses of Yahweh indeed never cease, for His compassions never fail. They are new every morning; great is Your faithfulness.

LAMENTATIONS 3:22-23

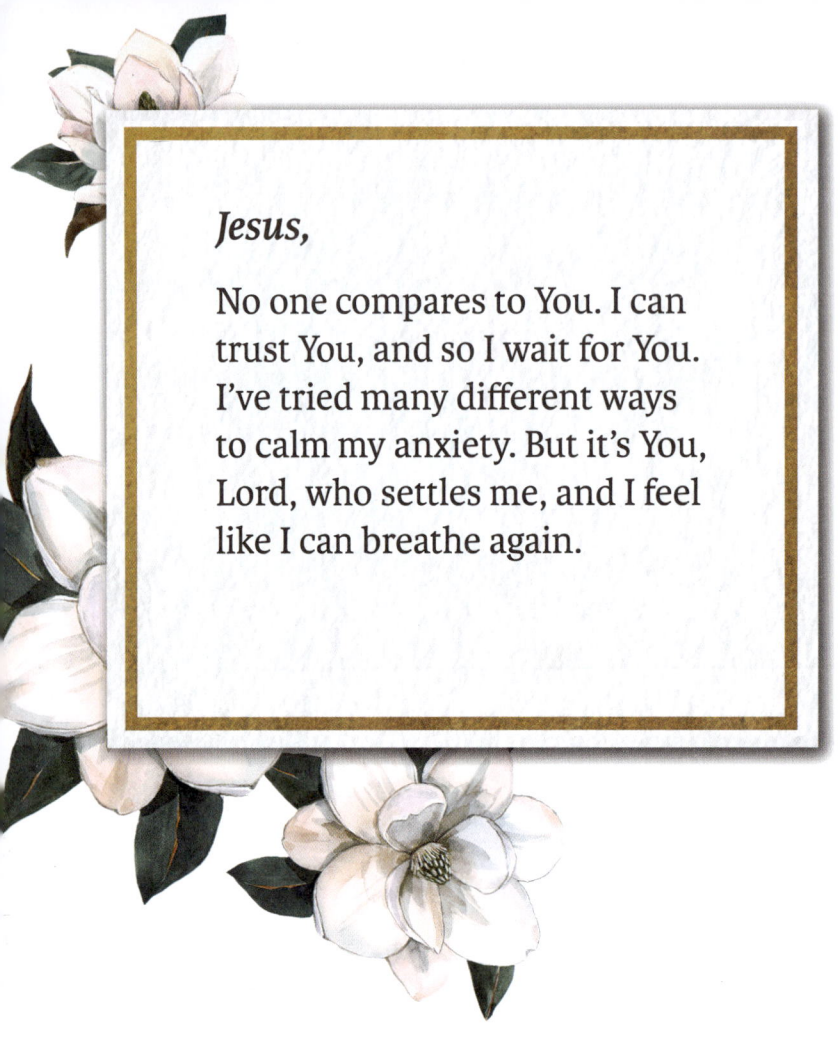

Jesus,

No one compares to You. I can trust You, and so I wait for You. I've tried many different ways to calm my anxiety. But it's You, Lord, who settles me, and I feel like I can breathe again.

Surely my soul waits in silence for God; from Him is my salvation.

PSALM 62:1

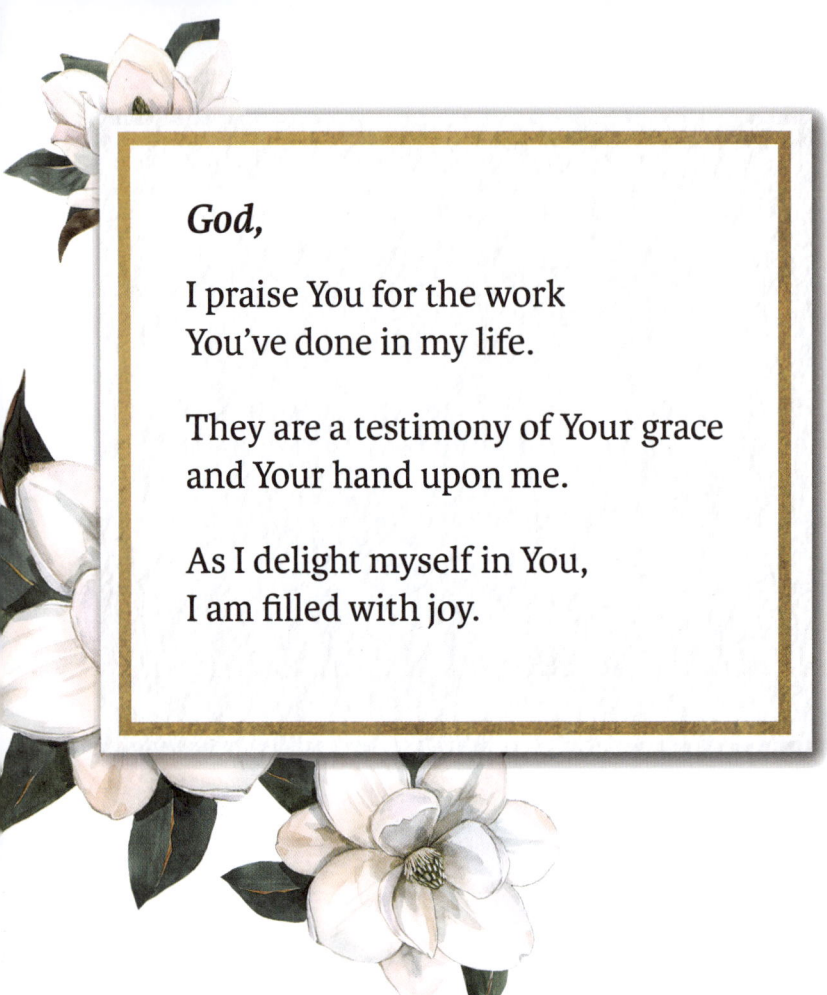

God,

I praise You for the work
You've done in my life.

They are a testimony of Your grace
and Your hand upon me.

As I delight myself in You,
I am filled with joy.

Your testimonies also are my delight;
they are my counselors.

PSALM 119:24

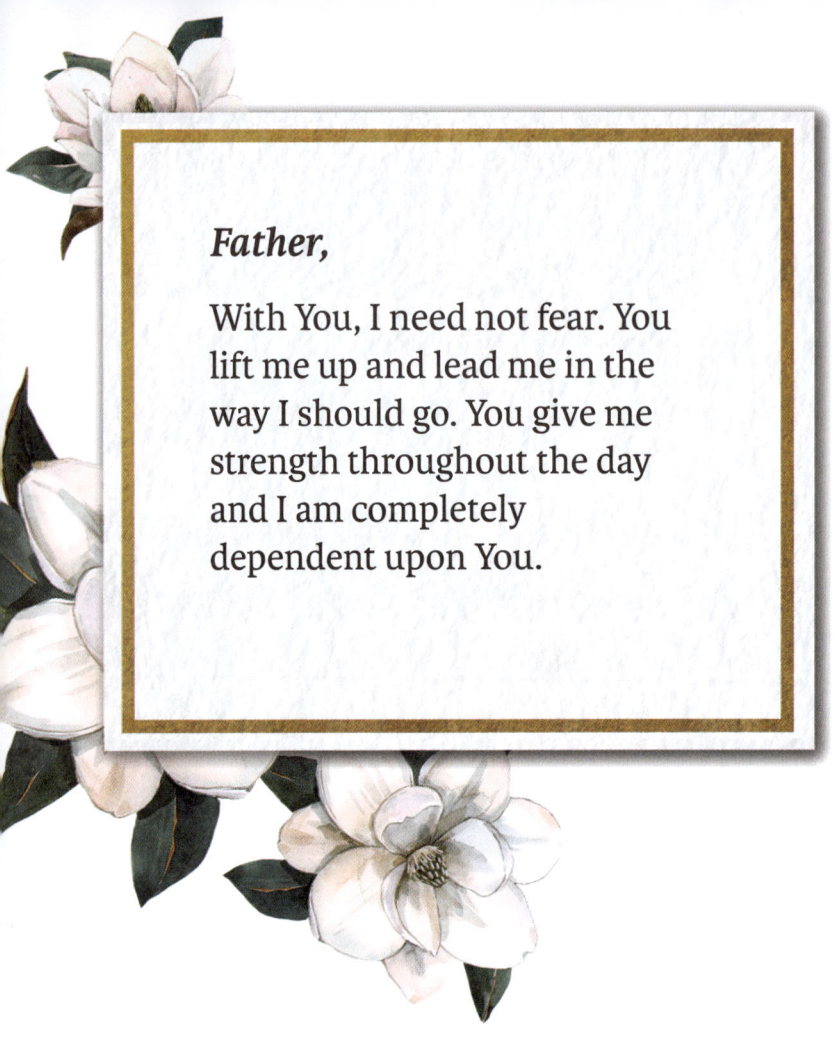

Father,

With You, I need not fear. You lift me up and lead me in the way I should go. You give me strength throughout the day and I am completely dependent upon You.

The LORD is my light and my salvation; whom shall I fear? The LORD is the defense of my life; whom shall I dread?

PSALM 27:1 NASB

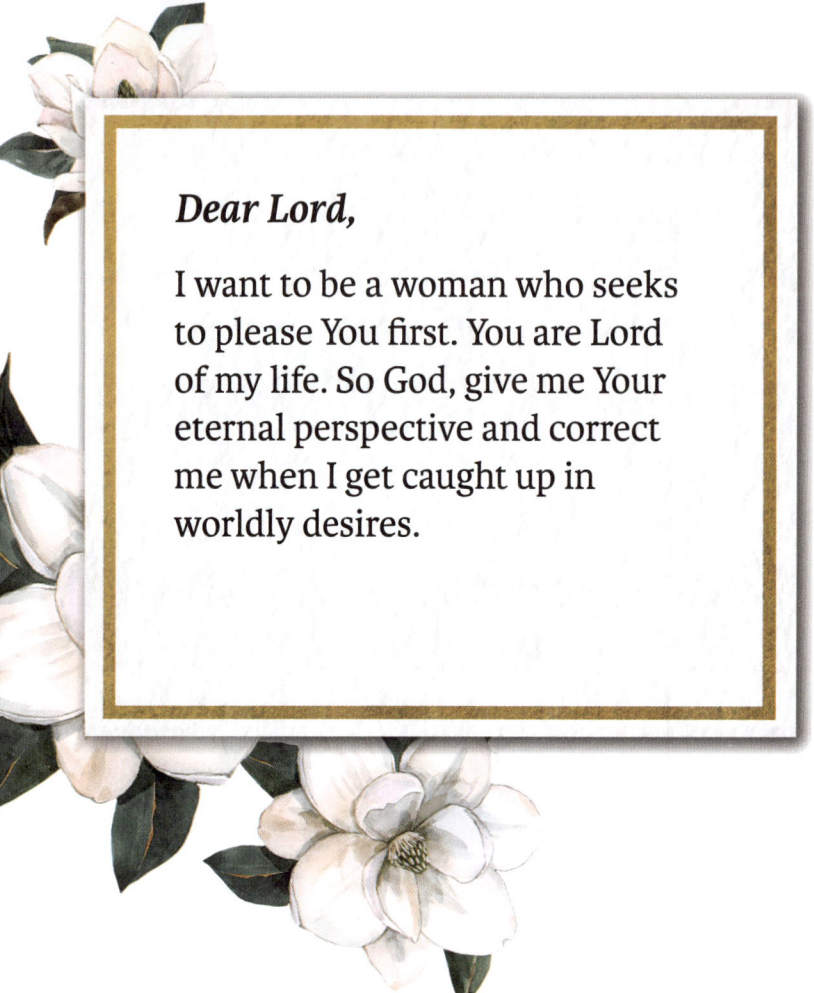

Dear Lord,

I want to be a woman who seeks to please You first. You are Lord of my life. So God, give me Your eternal perspective and correct me when I get caught up in worldly desires.

For where your treasure is, there your heart will be also.

LUKE 12:34

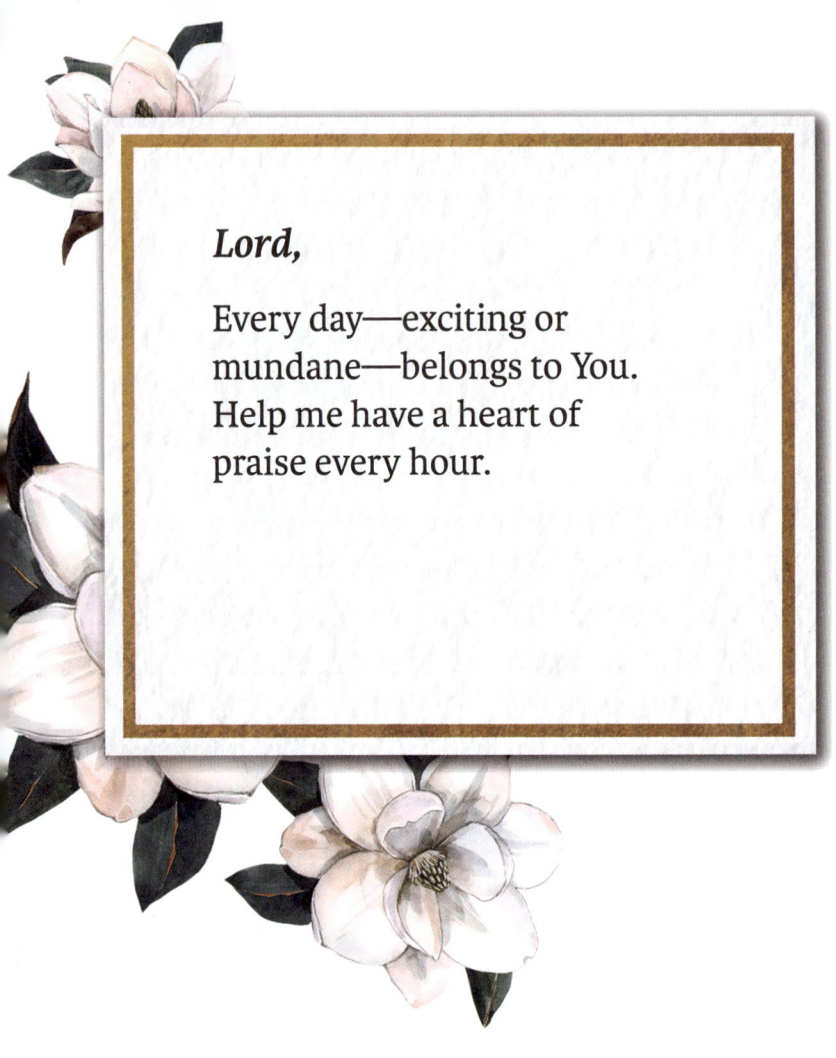

Lord,

Every day—exciting or mundane—belongs to You. Help me have a heart of praise every hour.

This is the day which the LORD has made; let us rejoice and be glad in it.

PSALM 118:24 NASB

O Lord,

I look to You as I continue on this journey. Life is not easy, and roadblocks often appear, but I set my gaze upon You, Lord. I have joy, because You have gone before me. I grab ahold of hope because You alone endured the cross. Thank You, Jesus.

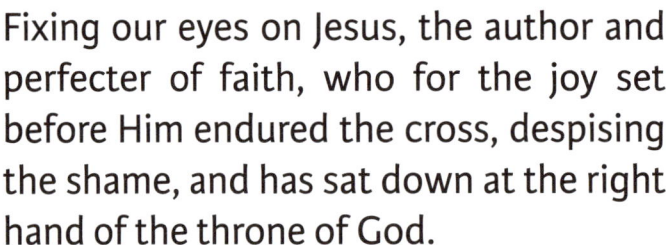

Fixing our eyes on Jesus, the author and perfecter of faith, who for the joy set before Him endured the cross, despising the shame, and has sat down at the right hand of the throne of God.

HEBREWS 12:2

Lord,

You are my Abba Father! Thank You that I can bring anything on my heart to You. Whether it's a personal praise or prayer, You are attentive to me.

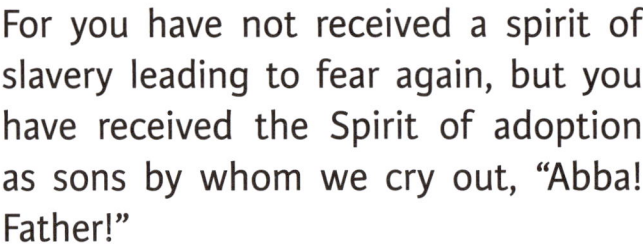

For you have not received a spirit of slavery leading to fear again, but you have received the Spirit of adoption as sons by whom we cry out, "Abba! Father!"

ROMANS 8:15

Heavenly Father,

Help me to forgive. When old feelings of bitterness hit me, Lord, please remove them. Jesus You've forgiven me, I need to forgive, too.

Let all bitterness and anger and wrath and shouting and slander be put away from you, along with all malice. Instead, be kind to one another, tender-hearted, graciously forgiving each other, just as God in Christ also has graciously forgiven you.

EPHESIANS 4:31-32

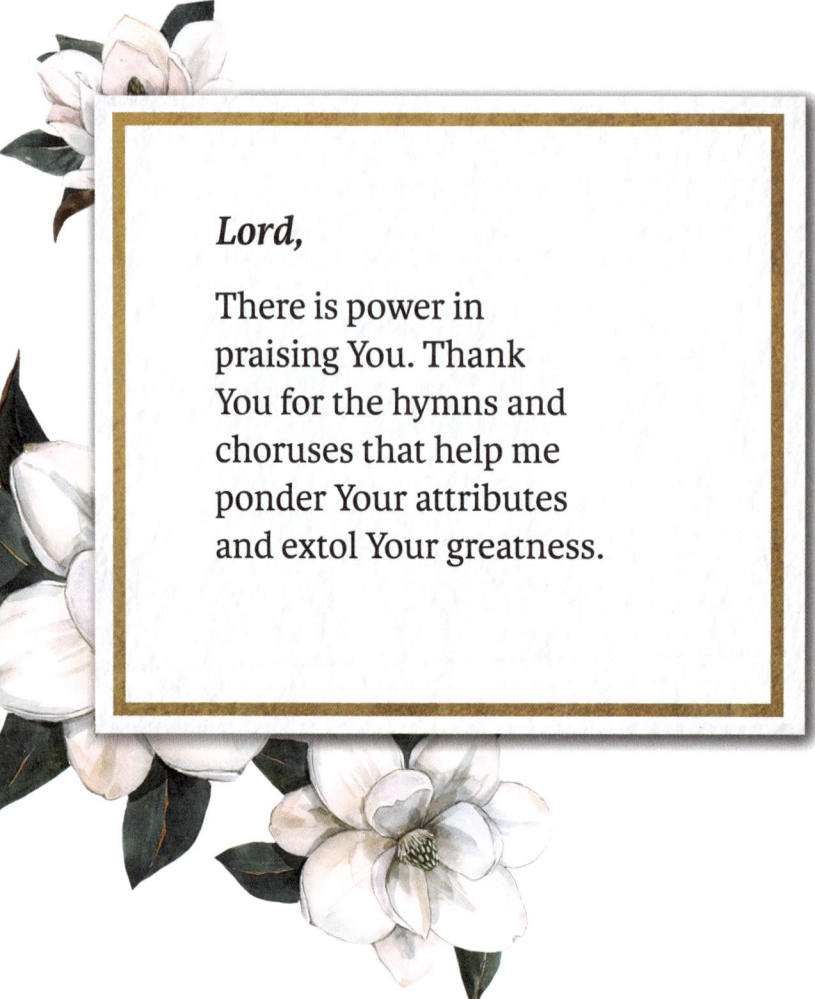

Lord,

There is power in praising You. Thank You for the hymns and choruses that help me ponder Your attributes and extol Your greatness.

Let the word of Christ dwell in you richly, with all wisdom teaching and admonishing one another with psalms and hymns and spiritual songs, singing with gratefulness in your hearts to God.

COLOSSIANS 3:16

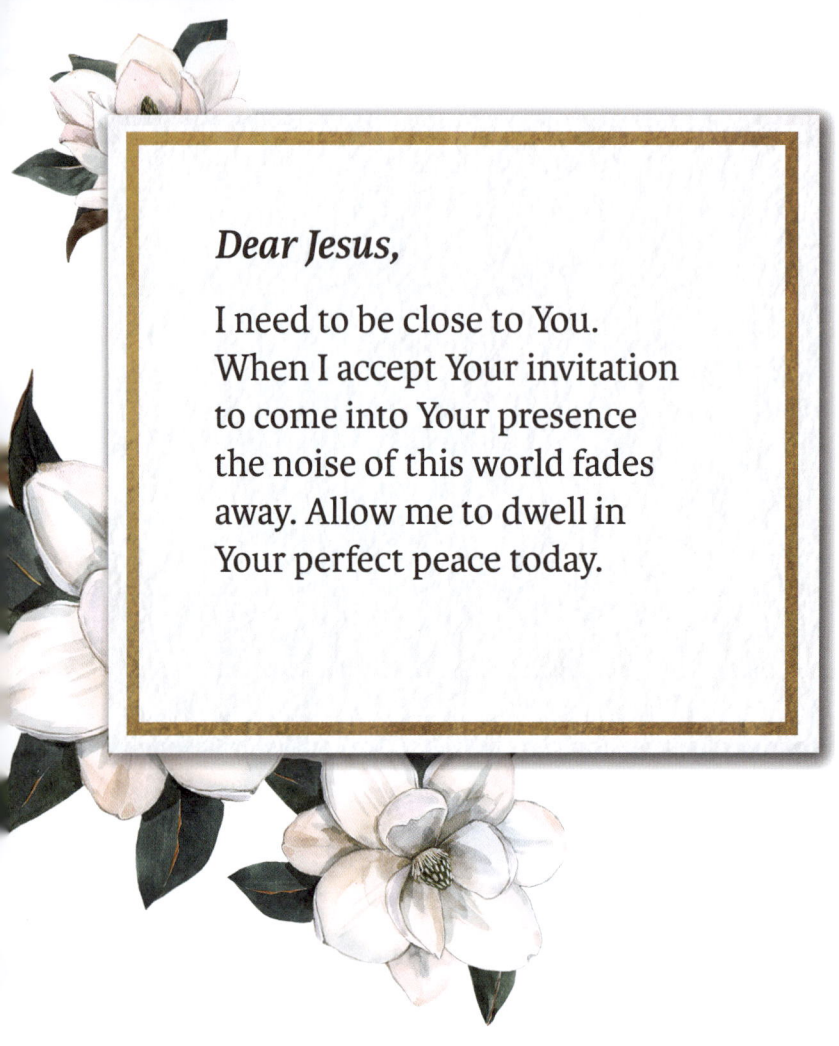

Dear Jesus,

I need to be close to You. When I accept Your invitation to come into Your presence the noise of this world fades away. Allow me to dwell in Your perfect peace today.

You drew near when I called on You; You said, "Do not fear!"

LAMENTATIONS 3:57

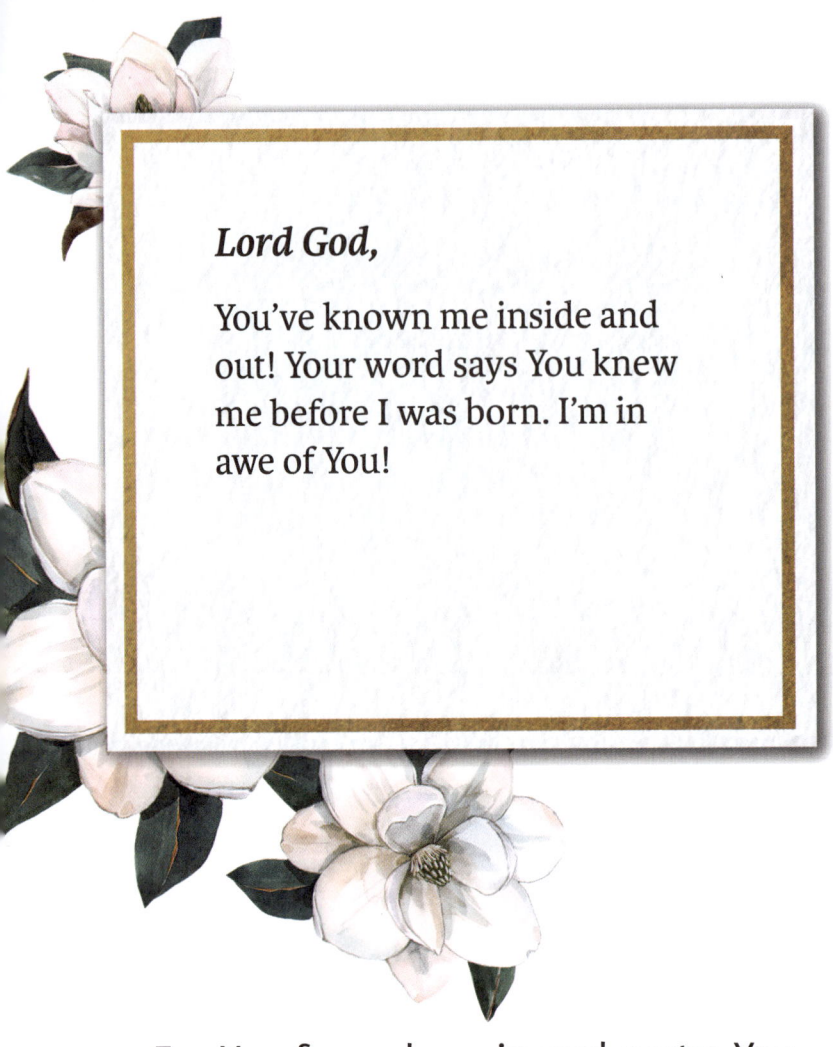

Lord God,

You've known me inside and out! Your word says You knew me before I was born. I'm in awe of You!

For You formed my inward parts; You wove me in my mother's womb. I will give thanks to You, for I am fearfully and wonderfully made; wonderful are Your works, and my soul knows it very well.

PSALM 139:13-14

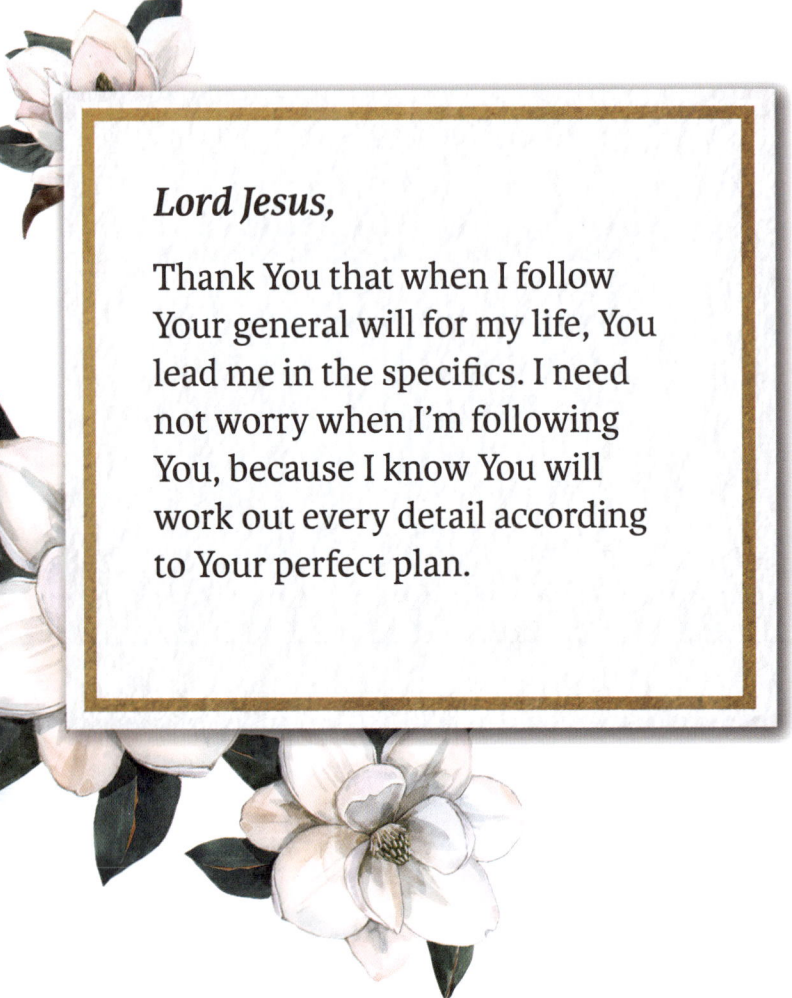

Lord Jesus,

Thank You that when I follow Your general will for my life, You lead me in the specifics. I need not worry when I'm following You, because I know You will work out every detail according to Your perfect plan.

But seek first His kingdom and His righteousness, and all these things will be added to you.

MATTHEW 6:33

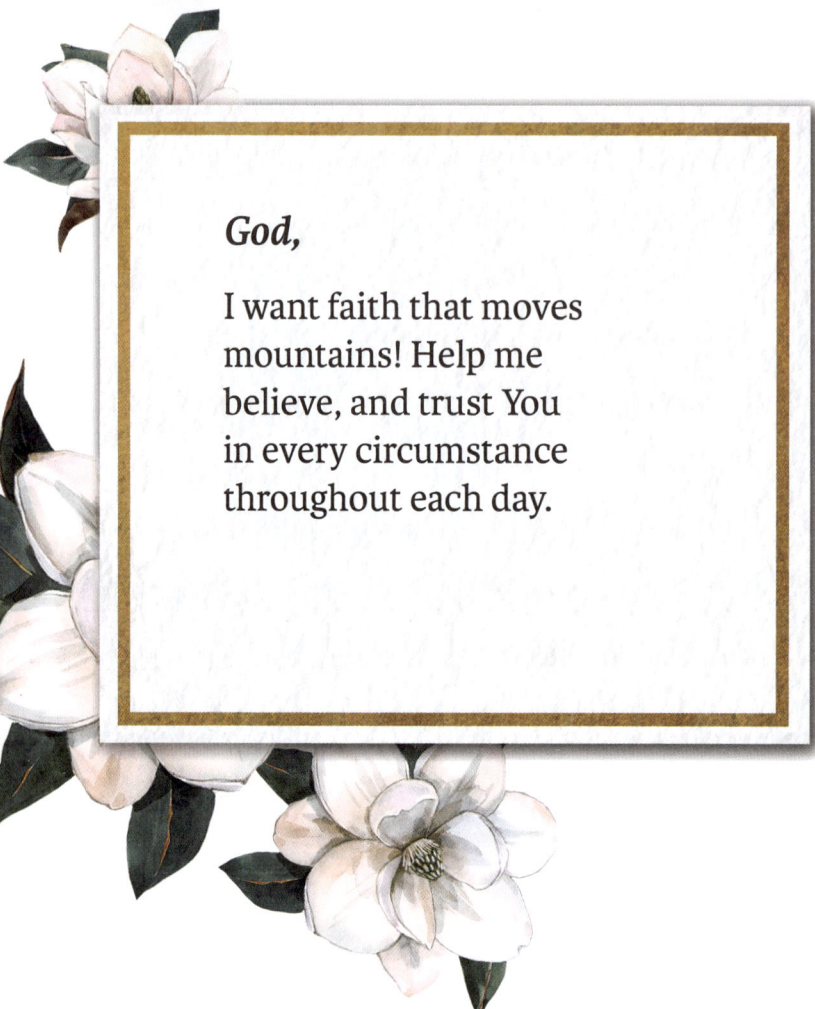

God,

I want faith that moves mountains! Help me believe, and trust You in every circumstance throughout each day.

Truly I say to you, whoever says to this mountain, "Be taken up and cast into the sea," and does not doubt in his heart, but believes that what he says is going to happen, it will be granted him.

MARK 11:23

Heavenly Father,

I worry about my loved ones who don't know You personally. You created them, so please help me turn my worries into trust! You love them even more than I do. Thank You, Lord, for Your promises, which never fail.

The Lord is not slow about His promise, as some consider slowness, but is patient toward you, not willing for any to perish but for all to come to repentance.

2 PETER 3:9

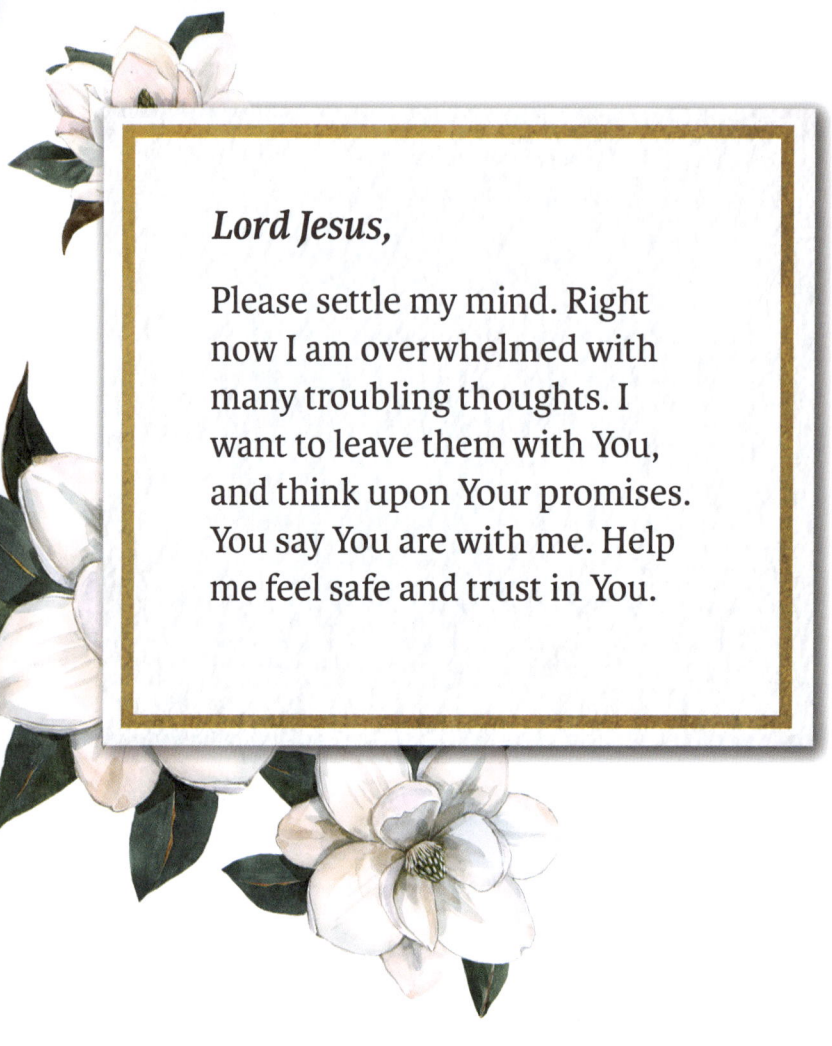

Lord Jesus,

Please settle my mind. Right now I am overwhelmed with many troubling thoughts. I want to leave them with You, and think upon Your promises. You say You are with me. Help me feel safe and trust in You.

The troubles of my heart are enlarged; bring me out of my distresses.

PSALM 25:17

Lord God,

You are my ever-present protector. I need not fear. You are always in control of all my days. Help me walk confidently in You!

The LORD will protect you from all evil; He will keep your soul. The LORD will guard your going out and your coming in from this time forth and forever.

PSALM 121:7-8 NASB

Lord,

There are days filled with well-worn paths of routine. In those places, help me to remember that I am Your ambassador wherever I am. May the Holy Spirit equip me to be ready to share the hope that You have given me through Your salvation.

So then, we are ambassadors for Christ, as God is pleading through us. We beg you on behalf of Christ, be reconciled to God.

2 CORINTHIANS 5:20

Heavenly Father,

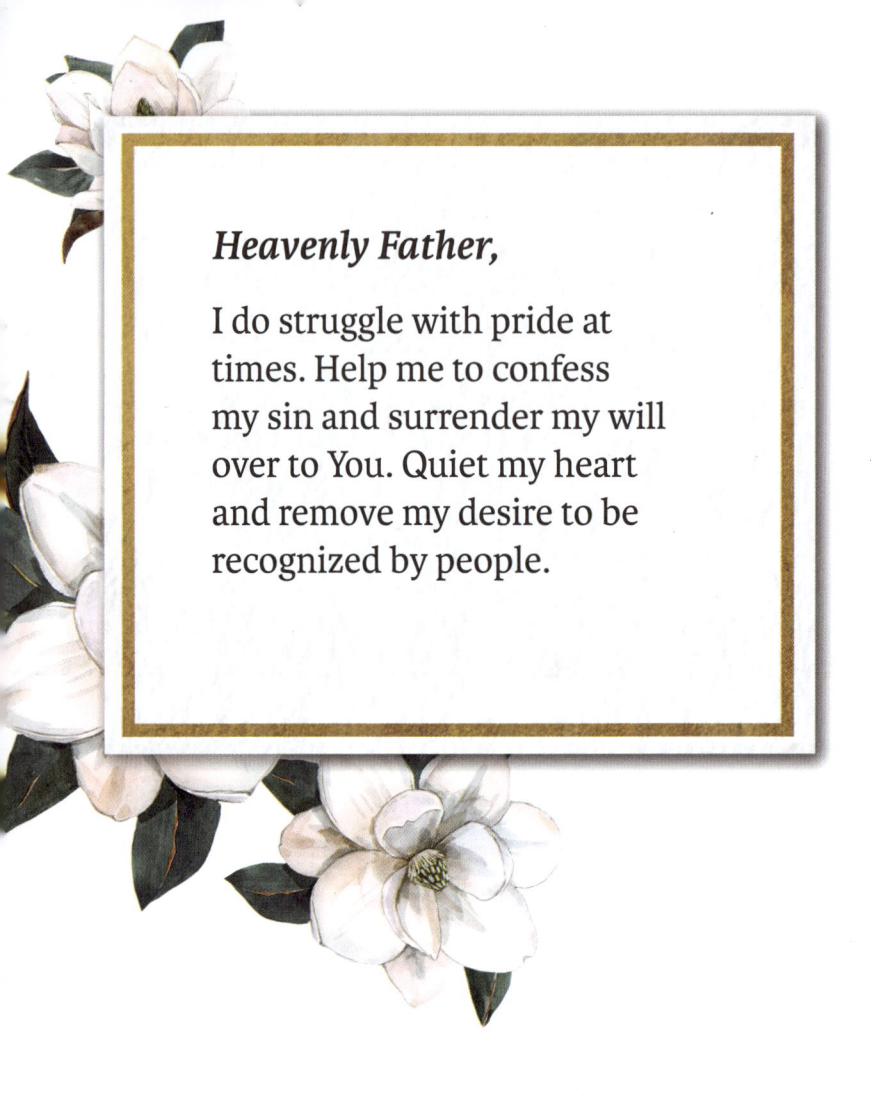

I do struggle with pride at times. Help me to confess my sin and surrender my will over to You. Quiet my heart and remove my desire to be recognized by people.

But He gives a greater grace. Therefore it says, "God is opposed to the proud, but gives grace to the humble."

JAMES 4:6

Dear Jesus,

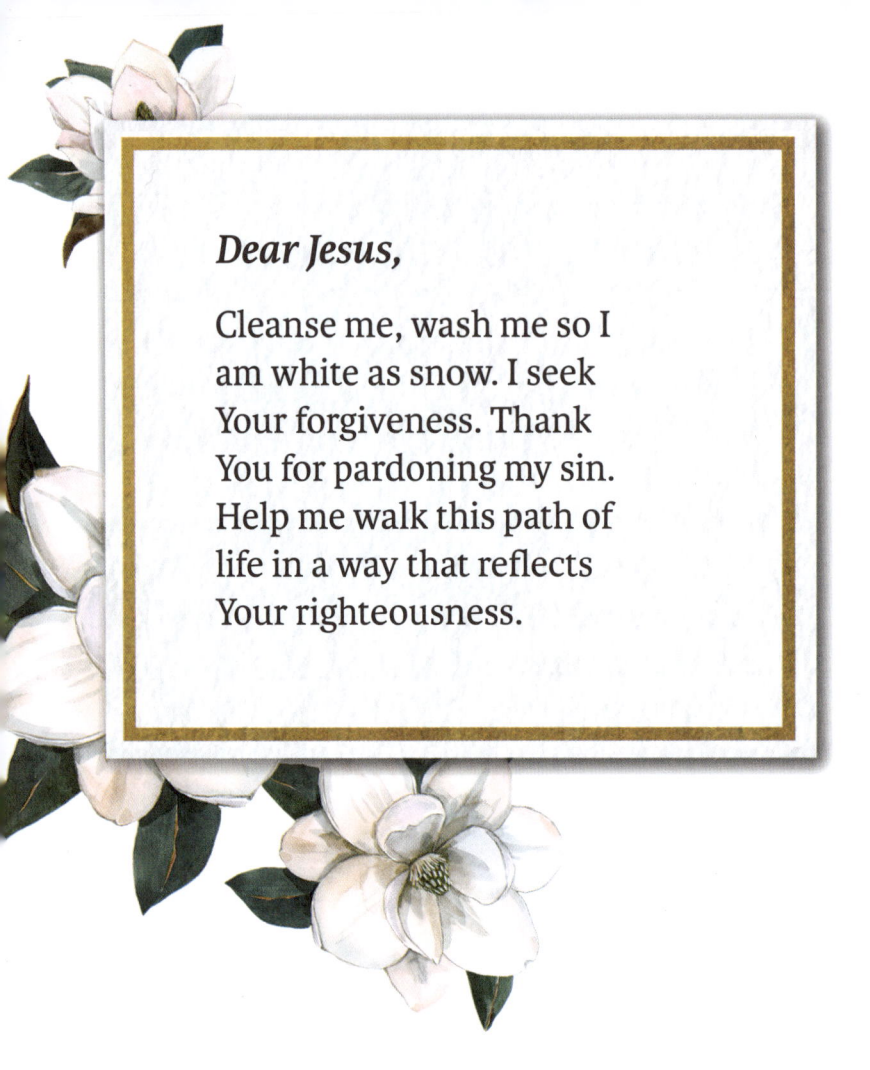

Cleanse me, wash me so I am white as snow. I seek Your forgiveness. Thank You for pardoning my sin. Help me walk this path of life in a way that reflects Your righteousness.

Search me, O God, and know my heart; try me and know my anxious thoughts; and see if there be any hurtful way in me, and lead me in the everlasting way.

PSALM 139:23-24

Jesus,

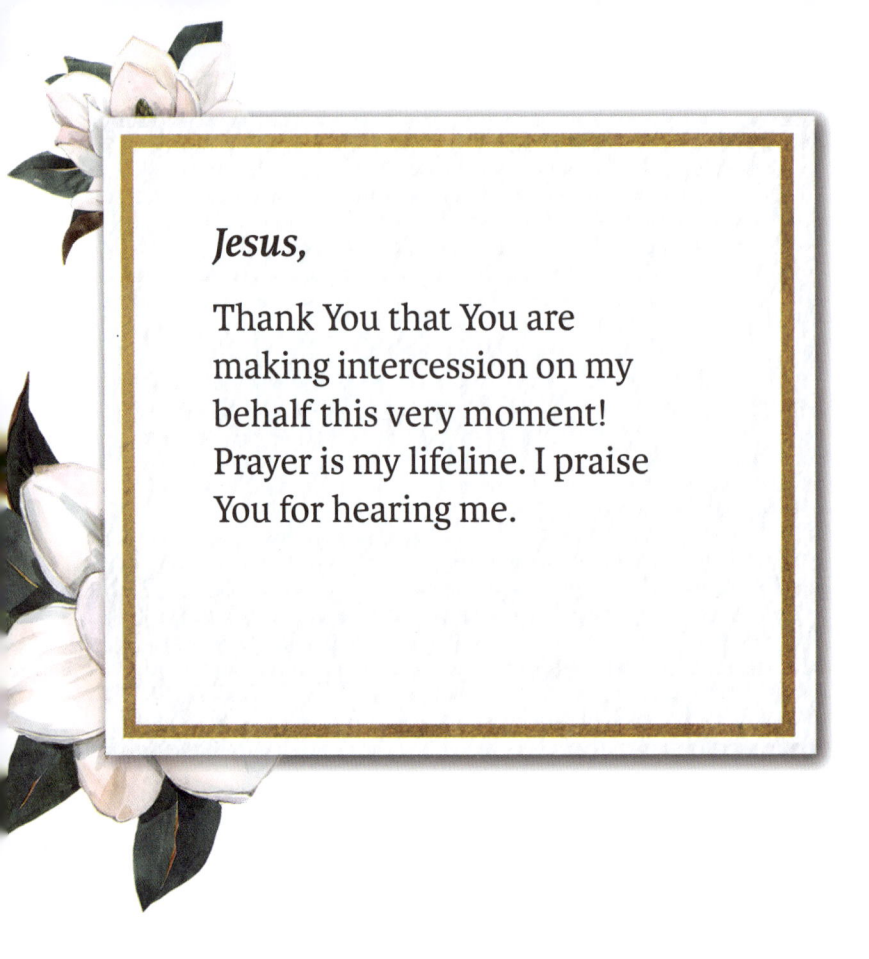

Thank You that You are making intercession on my behalf this very moment! Prayer is my lifeline. I praise You for hearing me.

Who will bring a charge against God's elect? God is the one who justifies; who is the one who condemns? Christ Jesus is He who died, yes, rather who was raised, who is at the right hand of God, who also intercedes for us.

ROMANS 8:33-34

Lord,

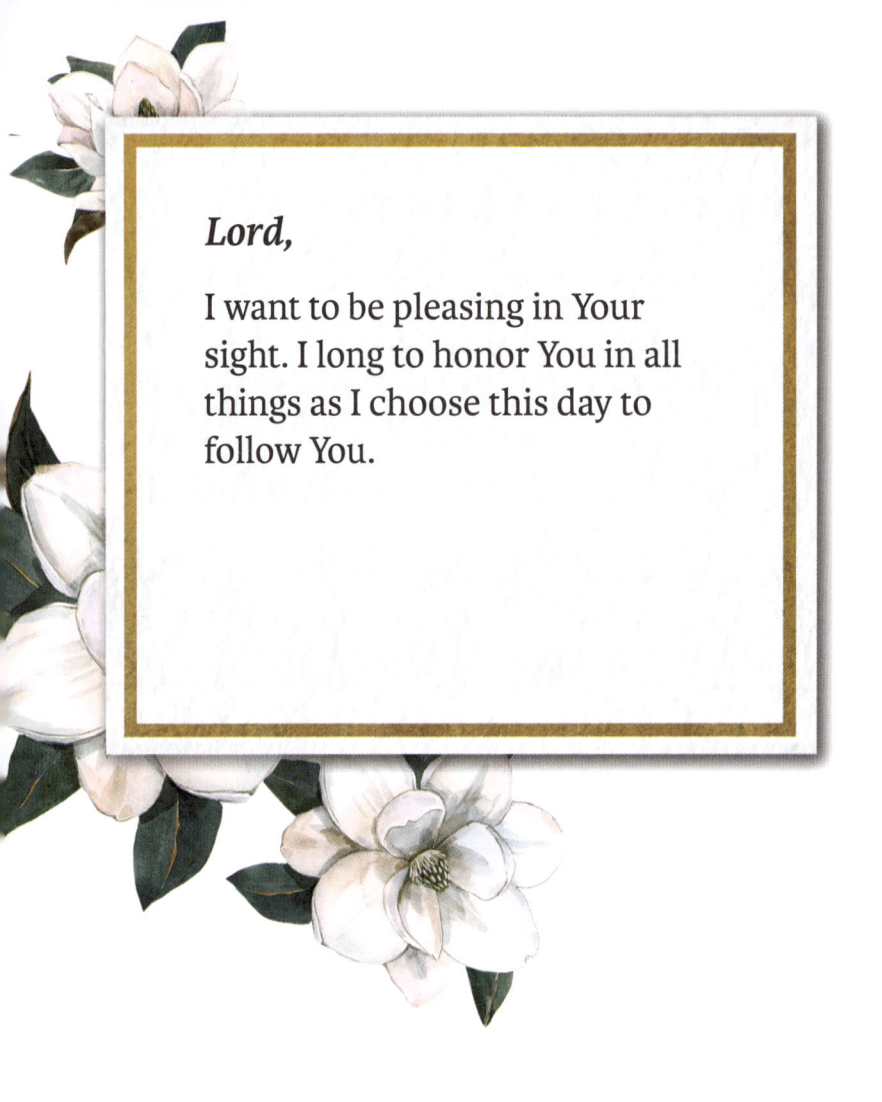

I want to be pleasing in Your sight. I long to honor You in all things as I choose this day to follow You.

Therefore we also have as our ambition, whether at home or absent, to be pleasing to Him.

2 CORINTHIANS 5:9

Father,

I want to be an example of godliness to others. Help me to have a gentle and quiet spirit—one that honors You. In this loud self-promoting world, cause my soul to be settled within, that I may hear Your still small voice.

Your adornment must not be merely external—braiding the hair, and wearing gold jewelry, or putting on garments; but let it be the hidden person of the heart, with the incorruptible quality of a lowly and quiet spirit, which is precious in the sight of God.

1 PETER 3:3-4

God,

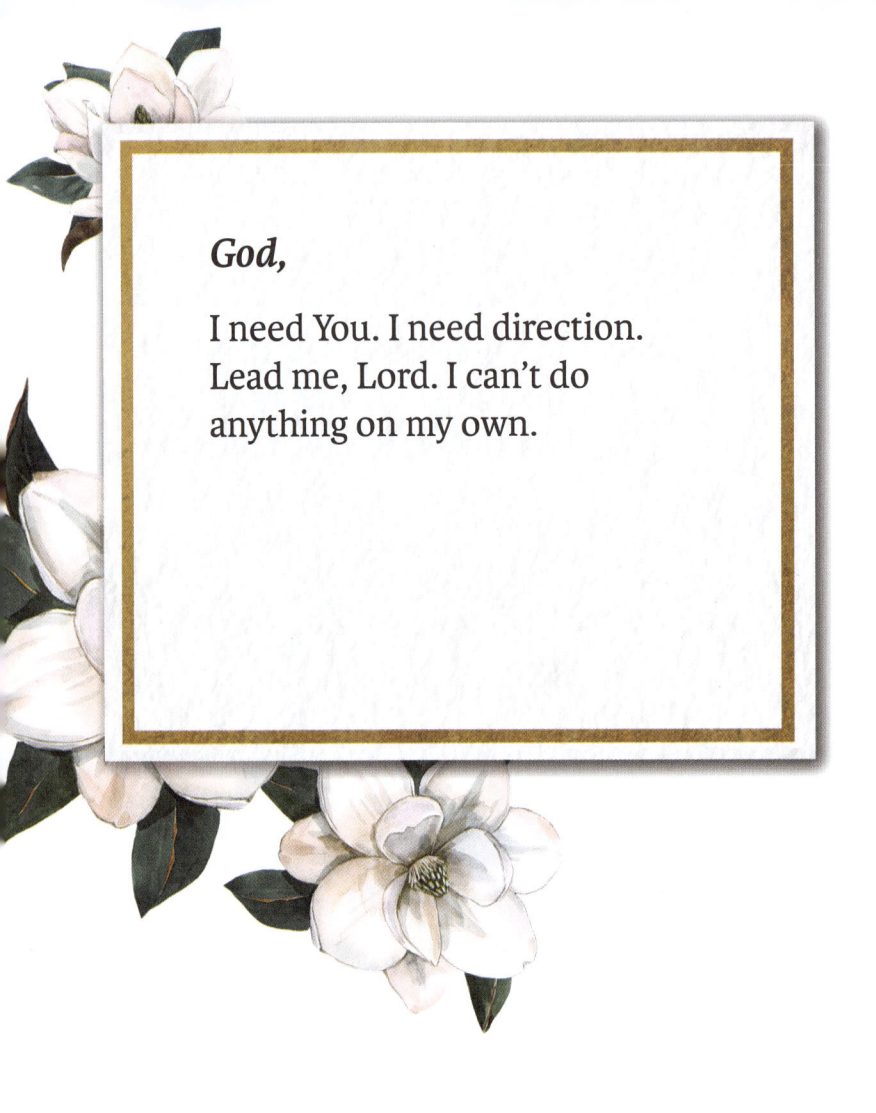

I need You. I need direction. Lead me, Lord. I can't do anything on my own.

For I am the LORD your God, who upholds your right hand, who says to you, "Do not fear, I will help you."

ISAIAH 41:13 NASB

Dear Jesus,

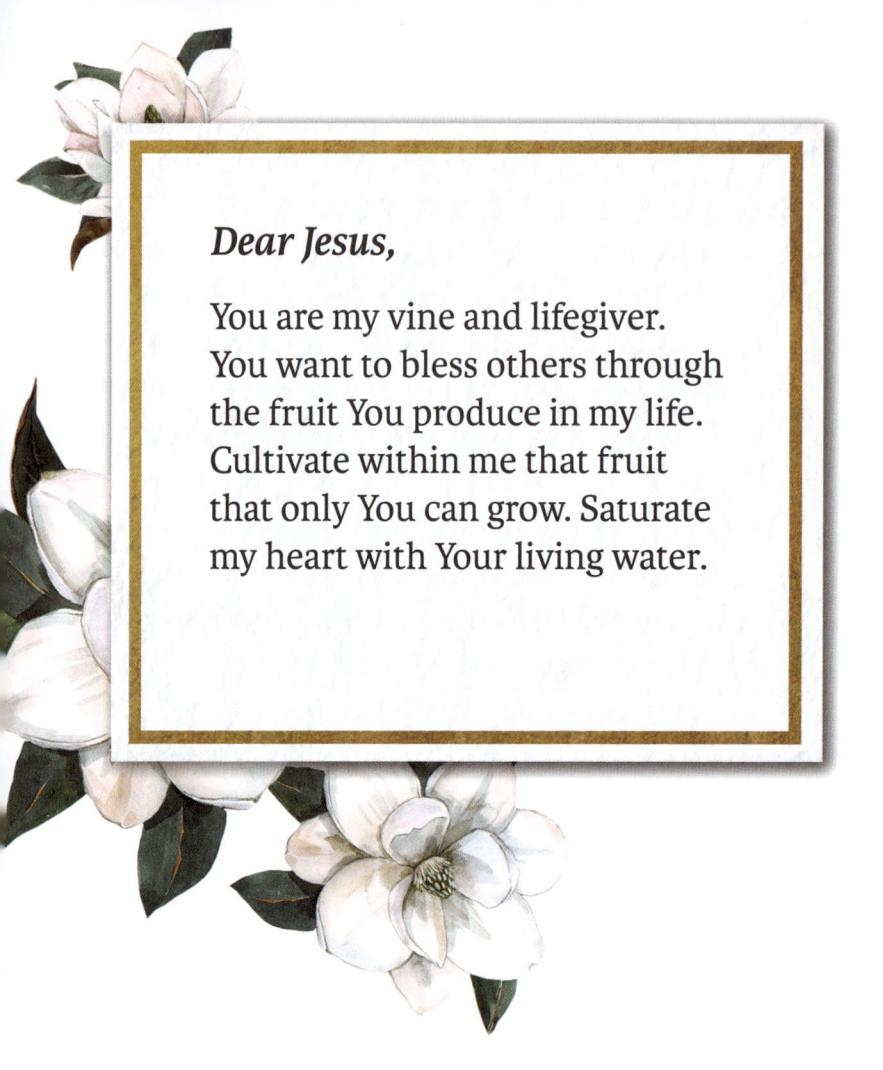

You are my vine and lifegiver. You want to bless others through the fruit You produce in my life. Cultivate within me that fruit that only You can grow. Saturate my heart with Your living water.

I am the vine, you are the branches; he who abides in Me and I in him, he bears much fruit, for apart from Me you can do nothing.

JOHN 15:5

Lord God,

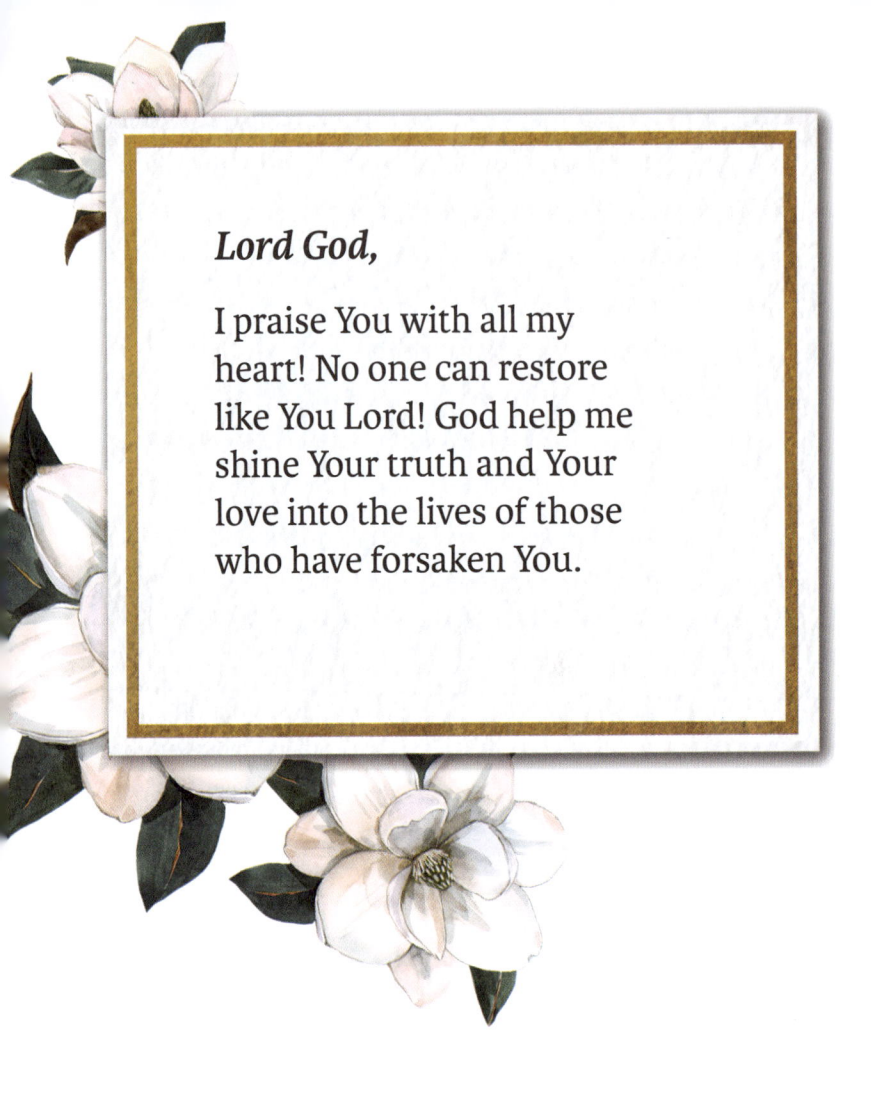

I praise You with all my heart! No one can restore like You Lord! God help me shine Your truth and Your love into the lives of those who have forsaken You.

He put a new song in my mouth, a song of praise to our God; many will see and fear and will trust in the LORD.

PSALM 40:3 NASB

Heavenly Father,

I've had sorrows, which You've carried me through. When I sense grief engulfing my heart, please lift me out of it. I'm in need of Your touch when sadness overwhelms me. I praise You for Your presence, which gives me comfort.

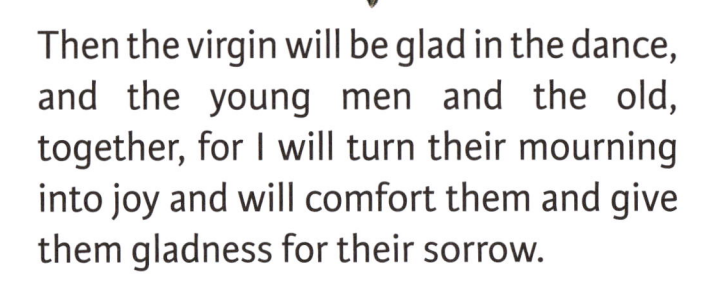

Then the virgin will be glad in the dance, and the young men and the old, together, for I will turn their mourning into joy and will comfort them and give them gladness for their sorrow.

JEREMIAH 31:13

God,

It's not difficult to remember the names of people who need You. Help me point the way to Jesus and may Your kindness lead them to repentance.

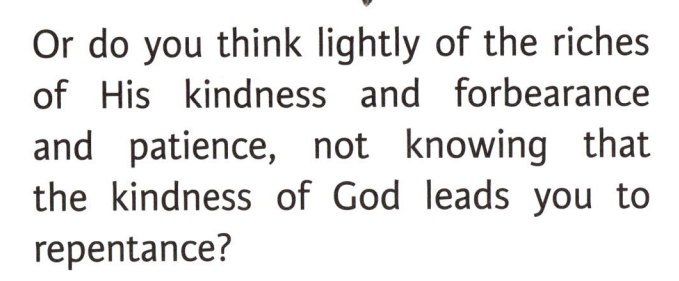

Or do you think lightly of the riches of His kindness and forbearance and patience, not knowing that the kindness of God leads you to repentance?

ROMANS 2:4

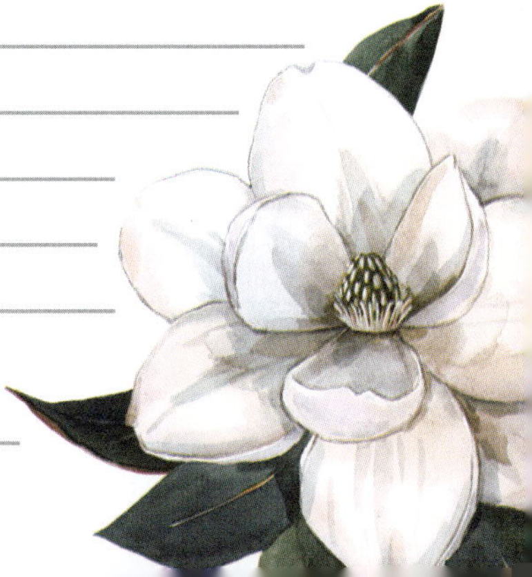

O Lord,

Help me to love like You do. When I see things in our culture that disturb me, cause me to pray. Give me boldness to share Your merciful truth with those I come in contact with. Merely complaining about it all is a waste of breath. Help me to see them how You do, Lord.

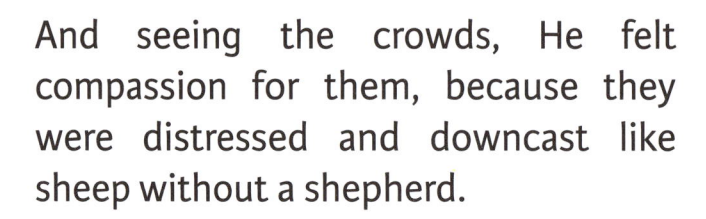

And seeing the crowds, He felt compassion for them, because they were distressed and downcast like sheep without a shepherd.

MATTHEW 9:36

Lord,

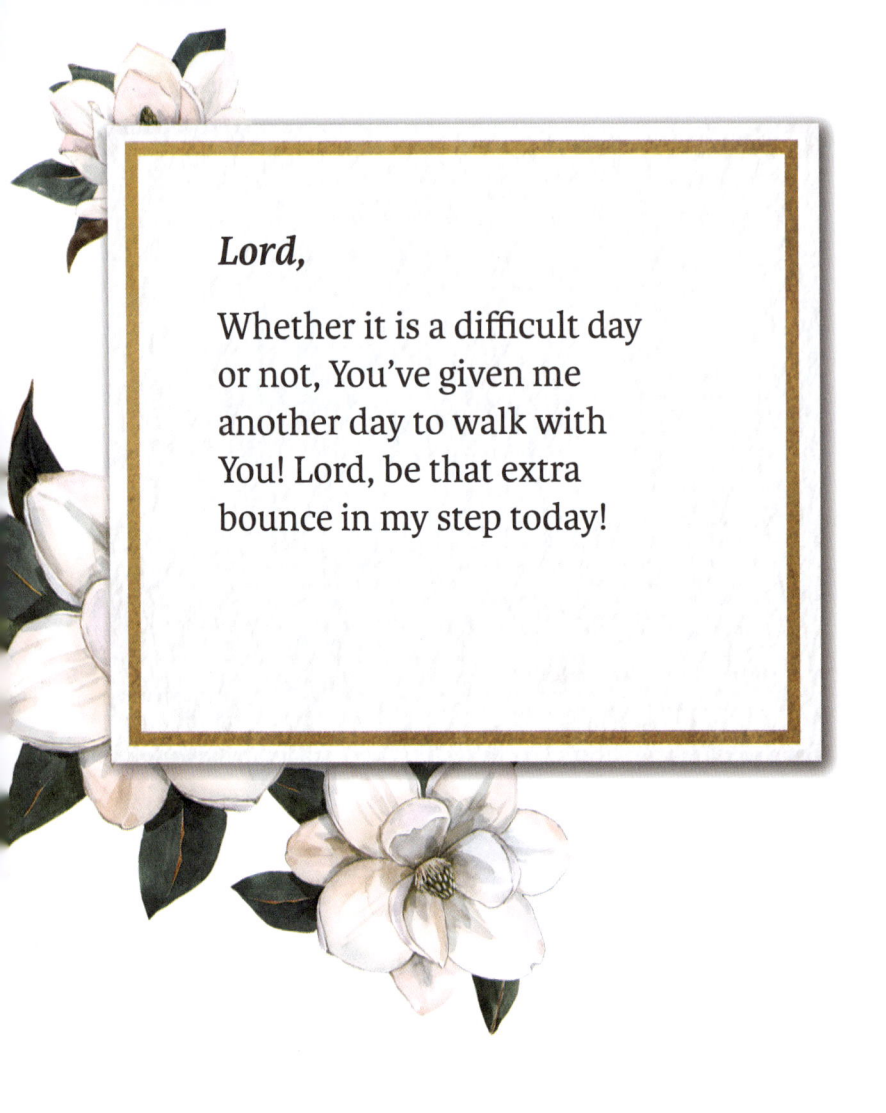

Whether it is a difficult day or not, You've given me another day to walk with You! Lord, be that extra bounce in my step today!

Rejoice in the Lord always; again I will say, rejoice!

PHILIPPIANS 4:4

Father,

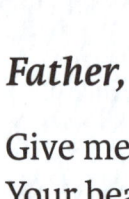

Give me eyes that recognize Your beauty that I often overlook. Even in common things like a dandelion I can discover the creative genius of Your design and praise You for it.

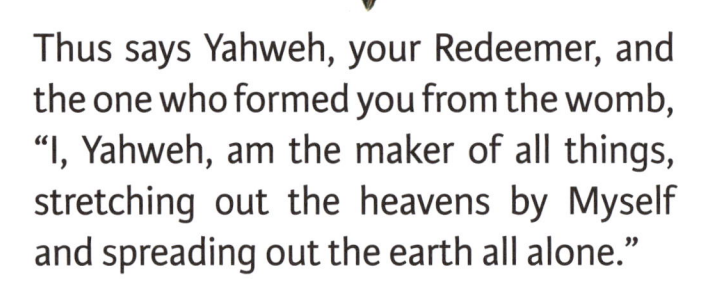

Thus says Yahweh, your Redeemer, and the one who formed you from the womb, "I, Yahweh, am the maker of all things, stretching out the heavens by Myself and spreading out the earth all alone."

ISAIAH 44:24

Lord,

Thank You for daily guiding me. I know I can trust You, even when I don't feel You. You are always faithful and good to Your children.

How great is Your goodness, which You have stored up for those who fear You, which You have worked for those who take refuge in You, before the sons of men!

PSALM 31:19

Dear Jesus,

Trials come and go. Thank You for leading me through each one. In Your perfect wisdom You use these seasons to strengthen me as I trust in You when life is difficult.

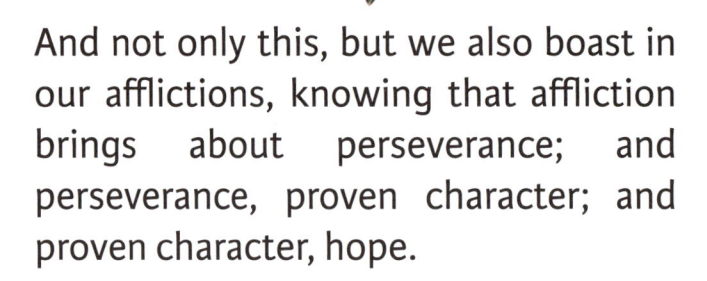

And not only this, but we also boast in our afflictions, knowing that affliction brings about perseverance; and perseverance, proven character; and proven character, hope.

ROMANS 5:3-4

Abba Father,

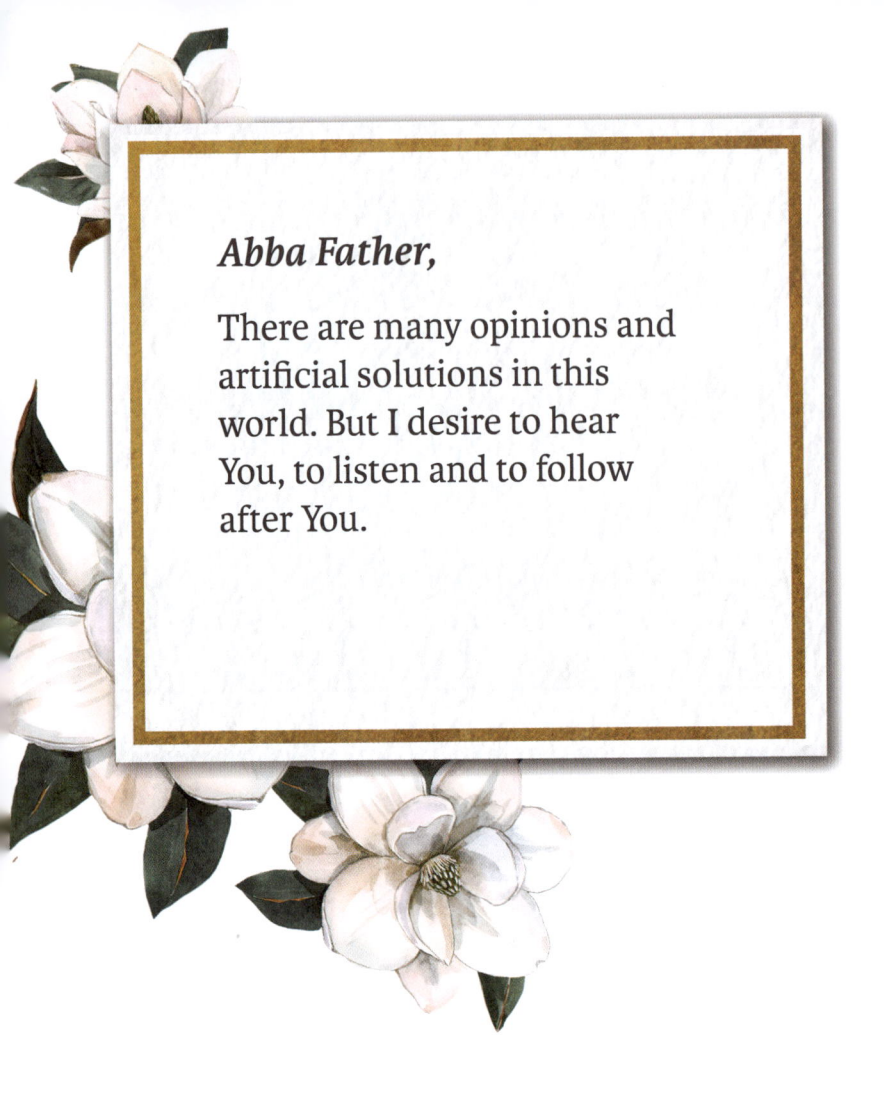

There are many opinions and artificial solutions in this world. But I desire to hear You, to listen and to follow after You.

But as for me, I will watch expectantly for the LORD; I will wait for the God of my salvation. My God will hear me.

MICAH 7:7 NASB

Lord,

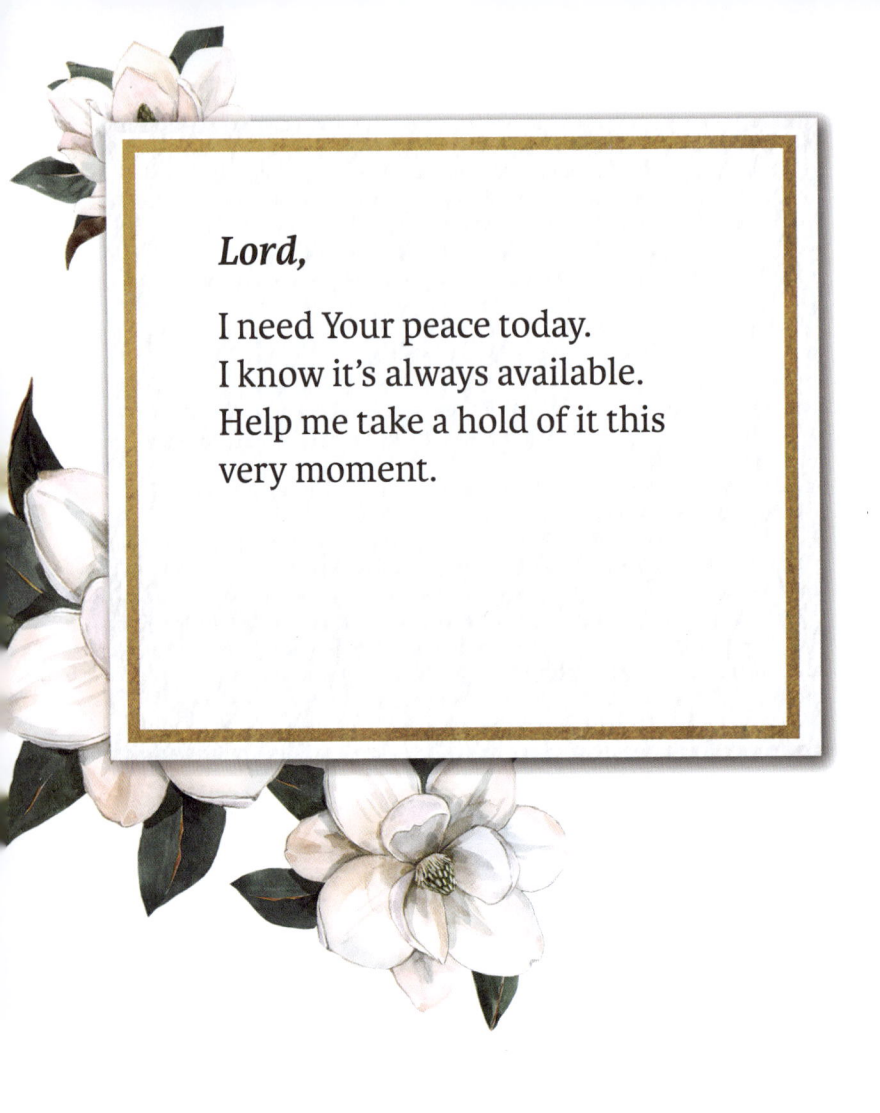

I need Your peace today.
I know it's always available.
Help me take a hold of it this
very moment.

Therefore, having been justified by faith, we have peace with God through our Lord Jesus Christ.

ROMANS 5:1

Heavenly Father,

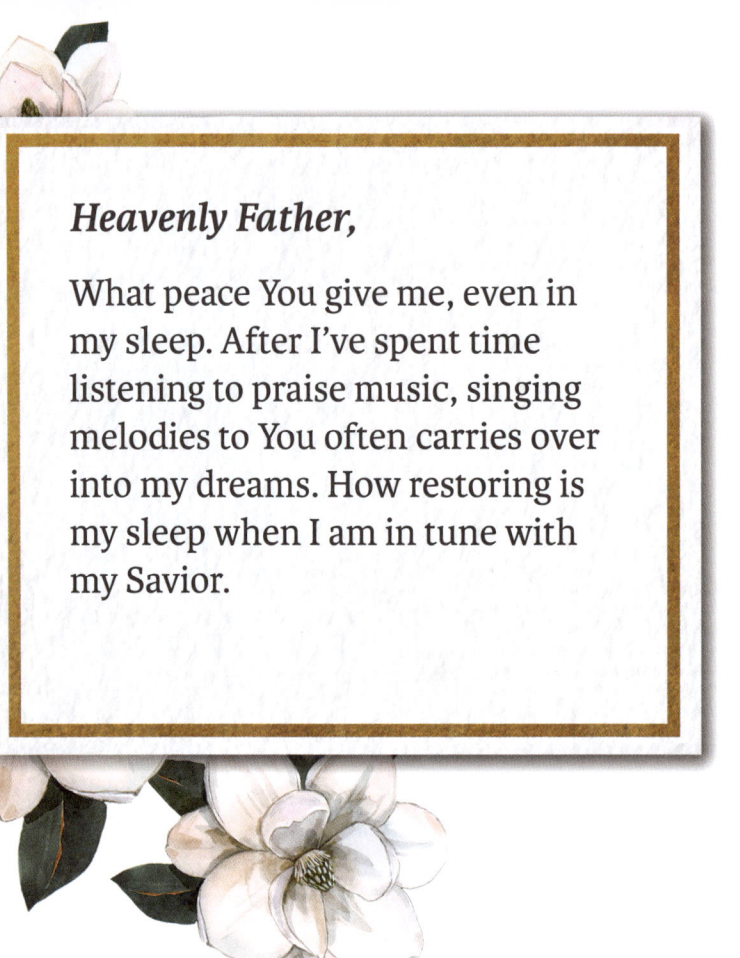

What peace You give me, even in my sleep. After I've spent time listening to praise music, singing melodies to You often carries over into my dreams. How restoring is my sleep when I am in tune with my Savior.

When you lie down, you will not be in dread; you will lie down, and your sleep will be pleasant.

PROVERBS 3:24

Lord God,

You plan the path laid out before me! I know You have gone ahead of me; so I follow You wholeheartedly.

You scrutinize my path and my lying down, and are intimately acquainted with all my ways.

PSALM 139:3

Dear Jesus,

There are times when I compare myself with others, which causes discontentment. I want to change my focus to all You have given me and respond with a grateful heart.

But godliness actually is a means of great gain, when accompanied by contentment. For we have brought nothing into the world, so we cannot take anything out of it either. And if we have food and covering, with these we shall be content.

1 TIMOTHY 6:6-8

Almighty God,

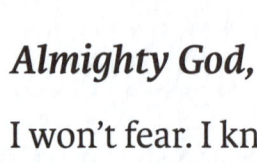

I won't fear. I know You are with me! I sense Your presence, even when darkness surrounds me. Lord, I will not fear. I'm putting my trust in You.

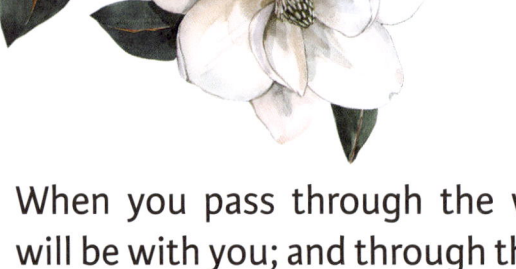

When you pass through the waters, I will be with you; and through the rivers, they will not overflow you. When you walk through the fire, you will not be scorched, nor will the flame burn you.

ISAIAH 43:2

Dear Jesus,

Life becomes busy and sometimes I forget about the cross. I am overly focused on the little wrongs done against me. Help me remember the price You paid, willingly for me. And also, help me to forgive those who have caused me pain, as You have forgiven me.

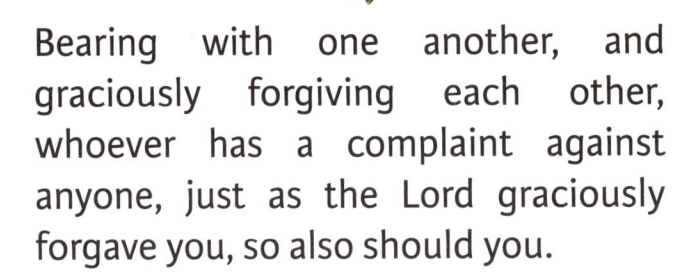

Bearing with one another, and graciously forgiving each other, whoever has a complaint against anyone, just as the Lord graciously forgave you, so also should you.

COLOSSIANS 3:13

Dear Jesus,

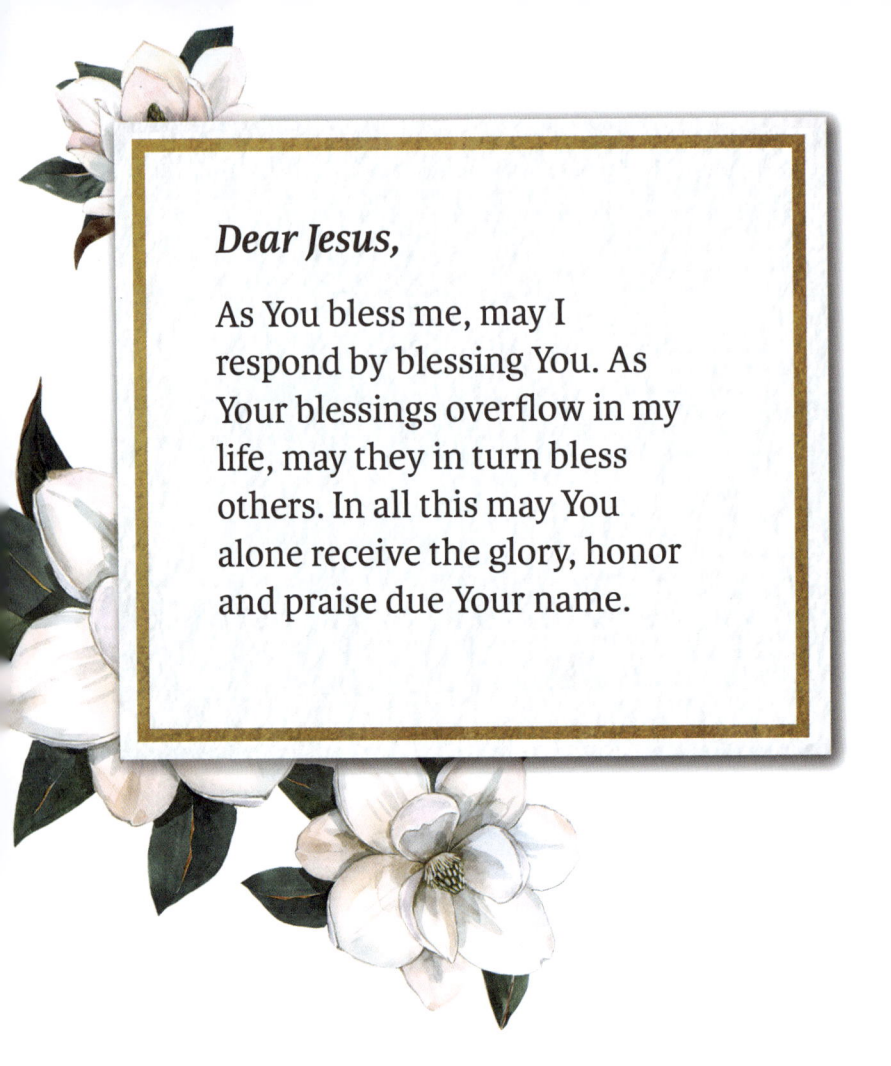

As You bless me, may I respond by blessing You. As Your blessings overflow in my life, may they in turn bless others. In all this may You alone receive the glory, honor and praise due Your name.

Amen, the blessing and the glory and the wisdom and the thanksgiving and the honor and the power and the strength, be to our God forever and ever. Amen.

REVELATION 7:12

Lord My Savior,

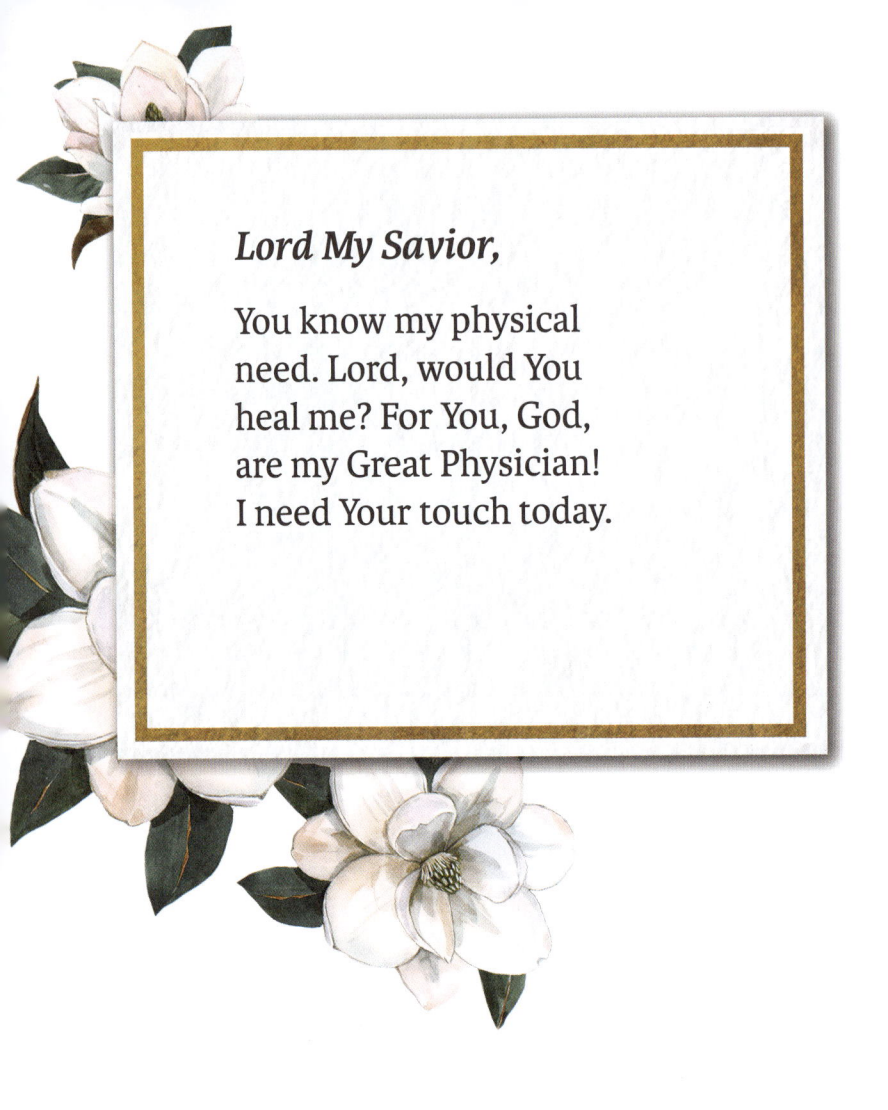

You know my physical need. Lord, would You heal me? For You, God, are my Great Physician! I need Your touch today.

For she was saying to herself, "If I only touch His garment, I will be saved from this."

MATTHEW 9:21

Lord God,

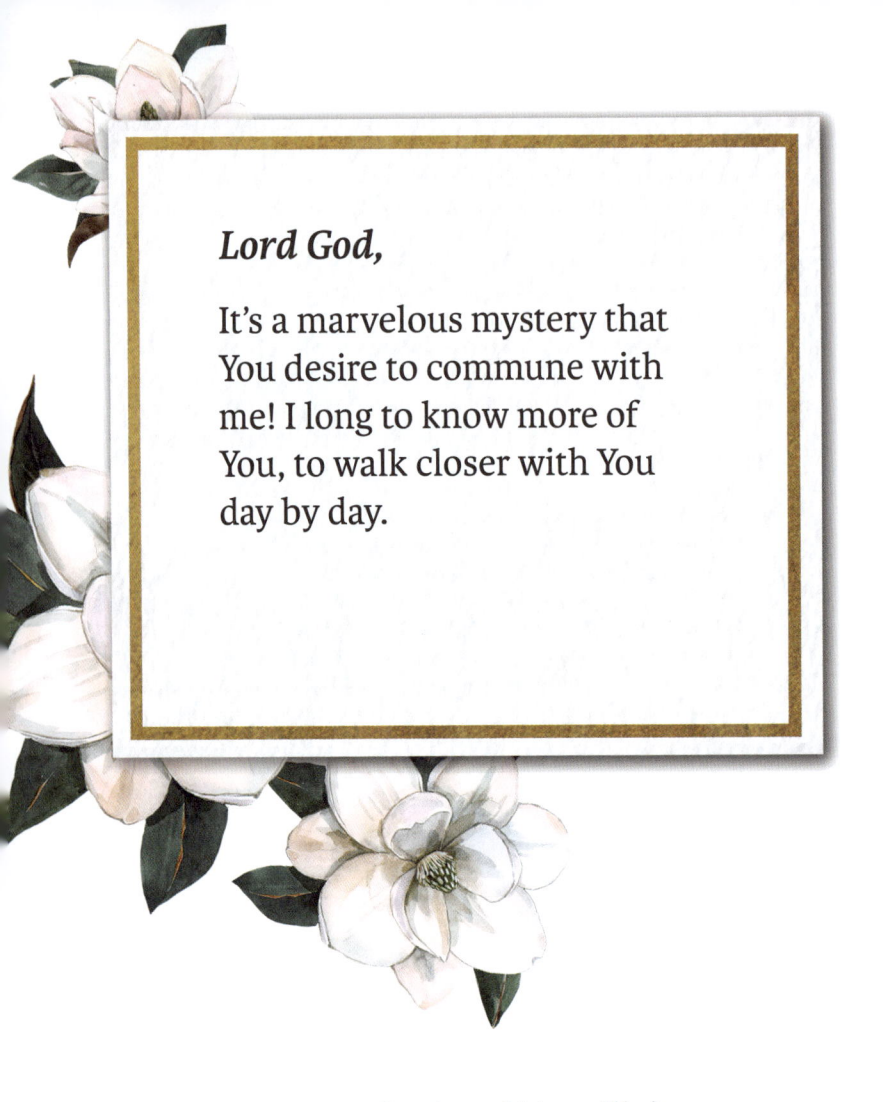

It's a marvelous mystery that You desire to commune with me! I long to know more of You, to walk closer with You day by day.

Draw near to God and He will draw near to you. Cleanse your hands, you sinners, and purify your hearts, you double-minded.

JAMES 4:8

Lord,

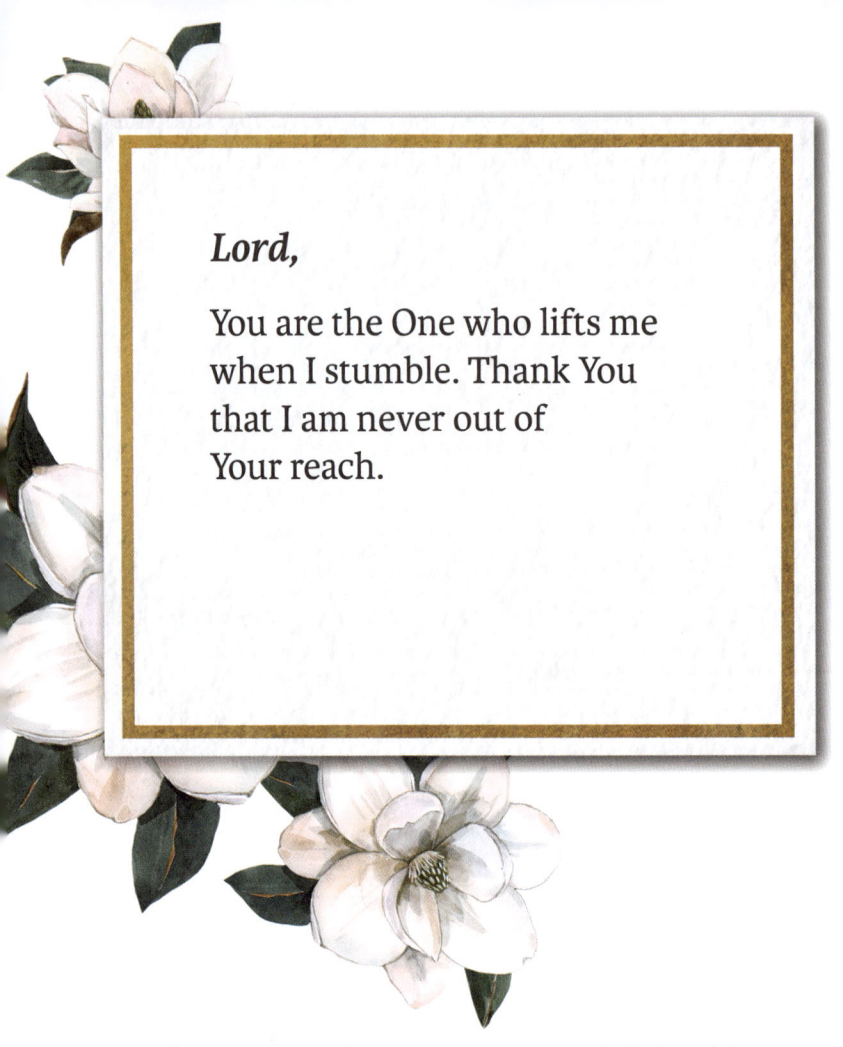

You are the One who lifts me when I stumble. Thank You that I am never out of Your reach.

The steps of a man are established by the LORD, and He delights in his way. When he falls, he will not be hurled headlong, because the LORD is the One who holds his hand.

PSALM 37:23-24 NASB

Lord,

Help me to lay down my own desires at Your feet and pick up my cross to follow You. May this be my prayer at the beginning of each day.

And He was saying to them all, "If anyone wishes to come after Me, let him deny himself, and take up his cross daily and follow Me."

LUKE 9:23

Lord God,

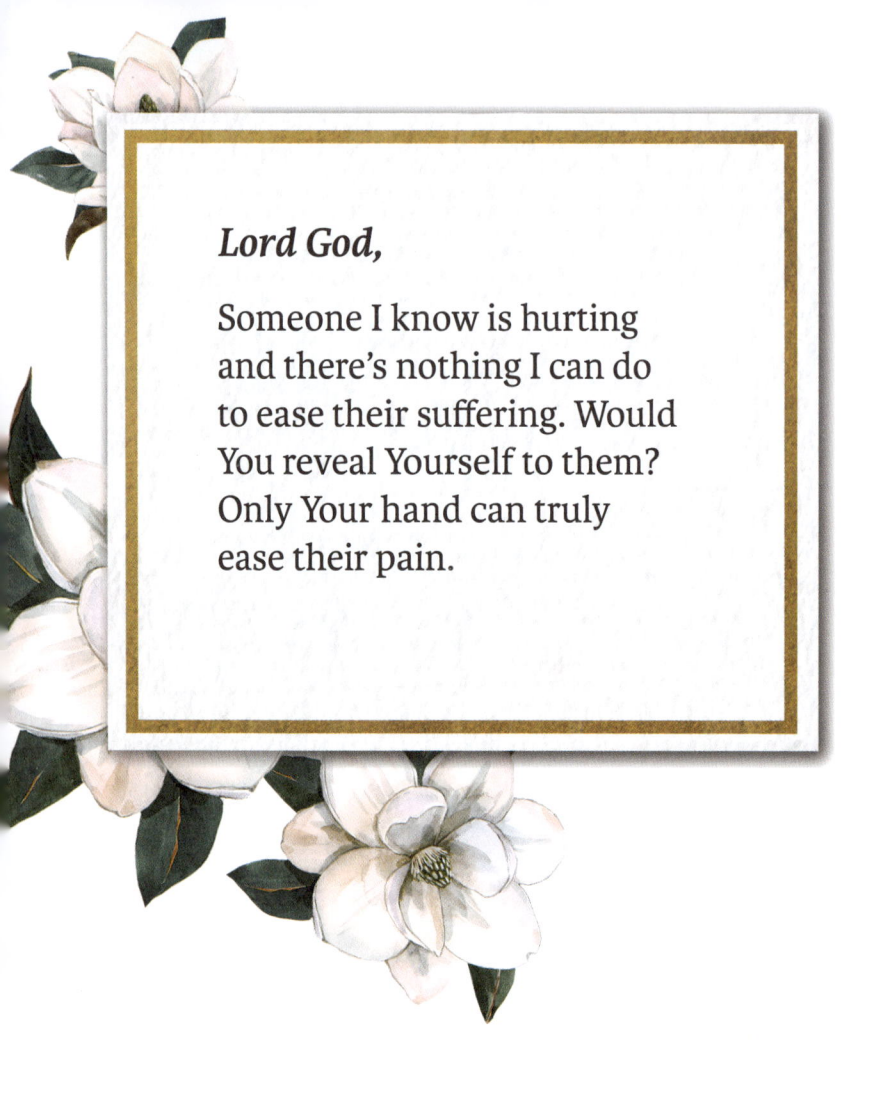

Someone I know is hurting and there's nothing I can do to ease their suffering. Would You reveal Yourself to them? Only Your hand can truly ease their pain.

Yahweh is near to the brokenhearted and saves those who are crushed in spirit.

PSALM 34:18

Lord God,

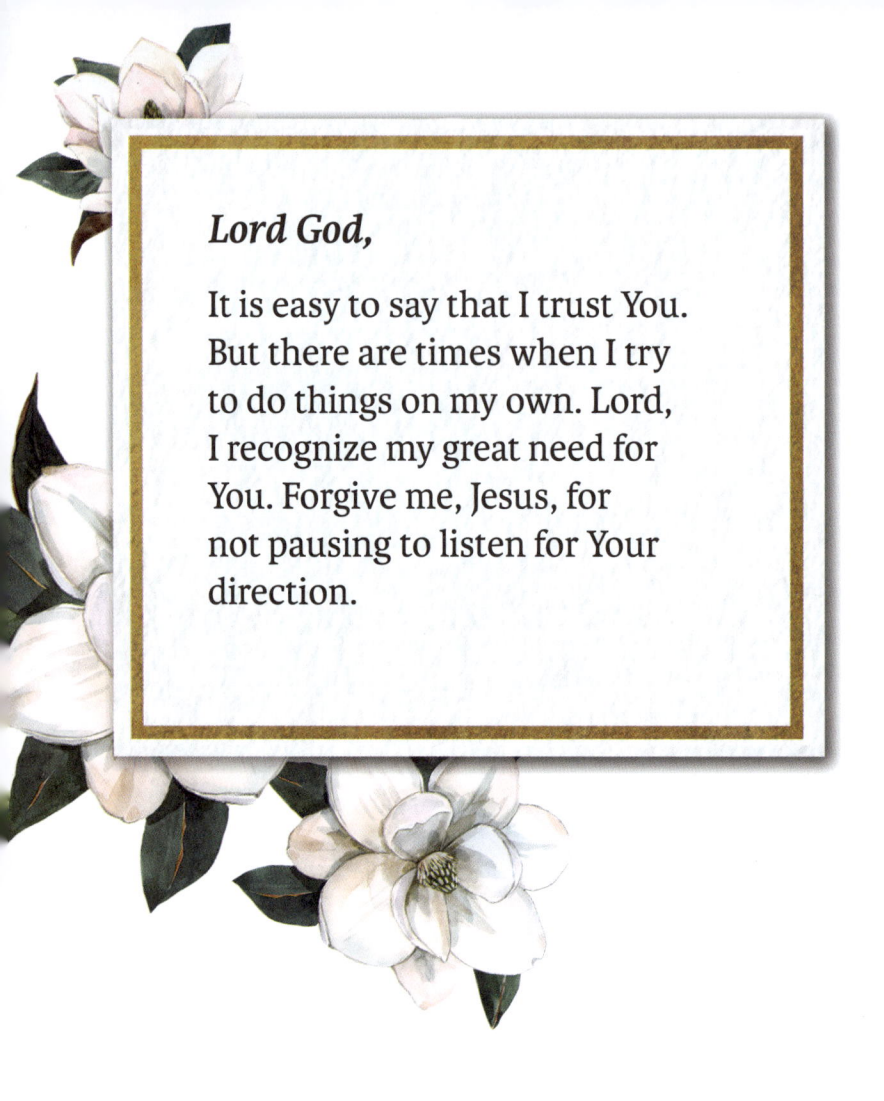

It is easy to say that I trust You. But there are times when I try to do things on my own. Lord, I recognize my great need for You. Forgive me, Jesus, for not pausing to listen for Your direction.

My sheep hear My voice, and I know them, and they follow Me.

JOHN 10:27

Lord Jesus,

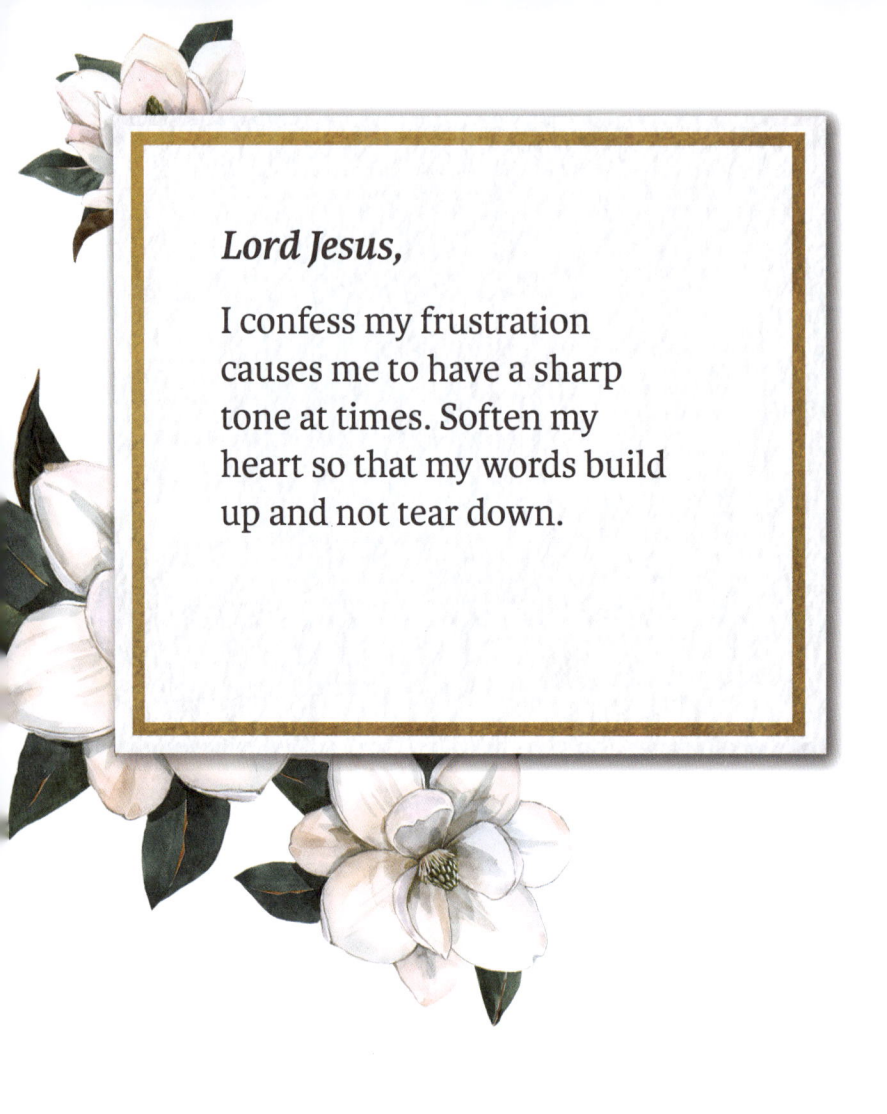

I confess my frustration causes me to have a sharp tone at times. Soften my heart so that my words build up and not tear down.

A gentle answer turns away wrath, but a harsh word stirs up anger.

PROVERBS 15:1

Lord,

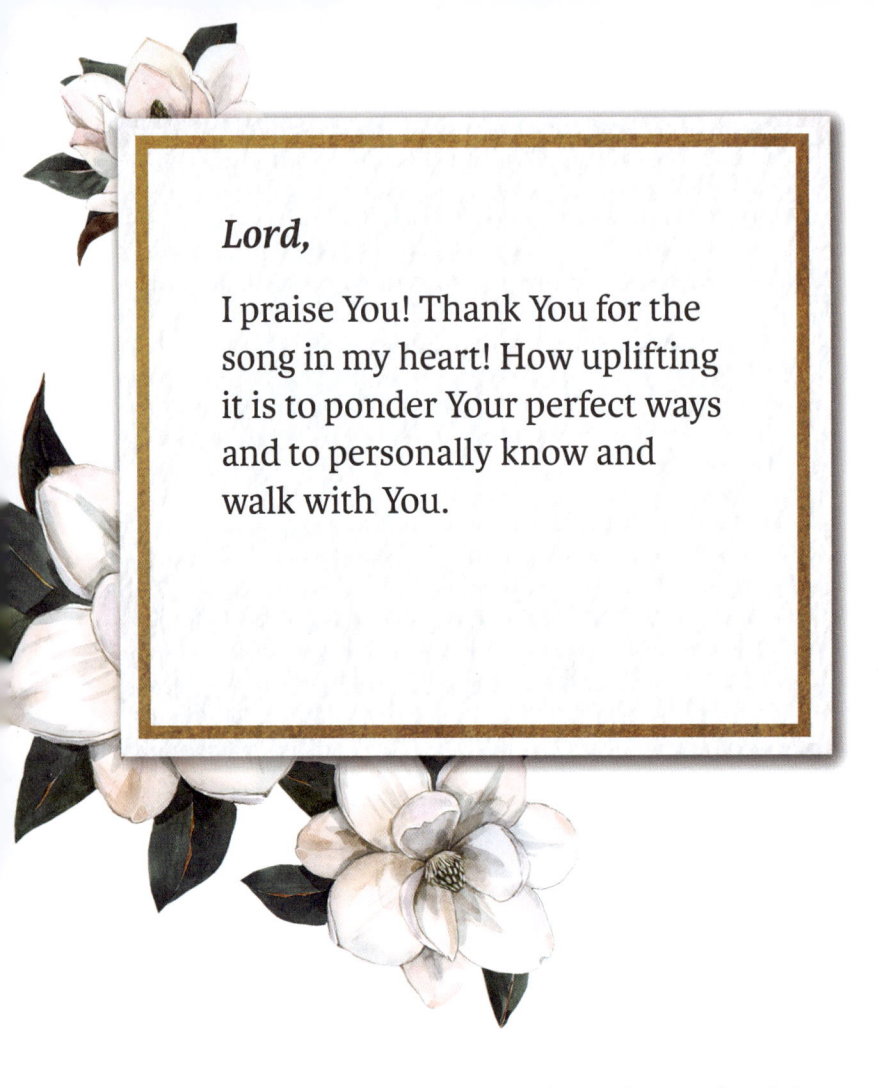

I praise You! Thank You for the song in my heart! How uplifting it is to ponder Your perfect ways and to personally know and walk with You.

The LORD is my strength and my shield; my heart trusts in Him, and I am helped; therefore my heart exults, and with my song I shall thank Him.

PSALM 28:7 NASB

Father,

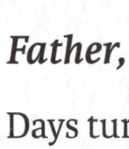

Days turn into weeks, and weeks turn into months. Time flies by, and before I know it, I've put the task You've given me on the backburner. Lord, I need Your focus to redeem the time, and Your Holy Spirit to guide me as I walk forward in faith.

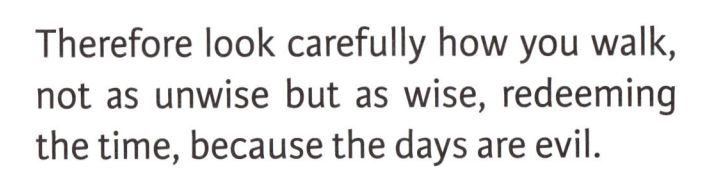

Therefore look carefully how you walk, not as unwise but as wise, redeeming the time, because the days are evil.

EPHESIANS 5:15-16

Father God,

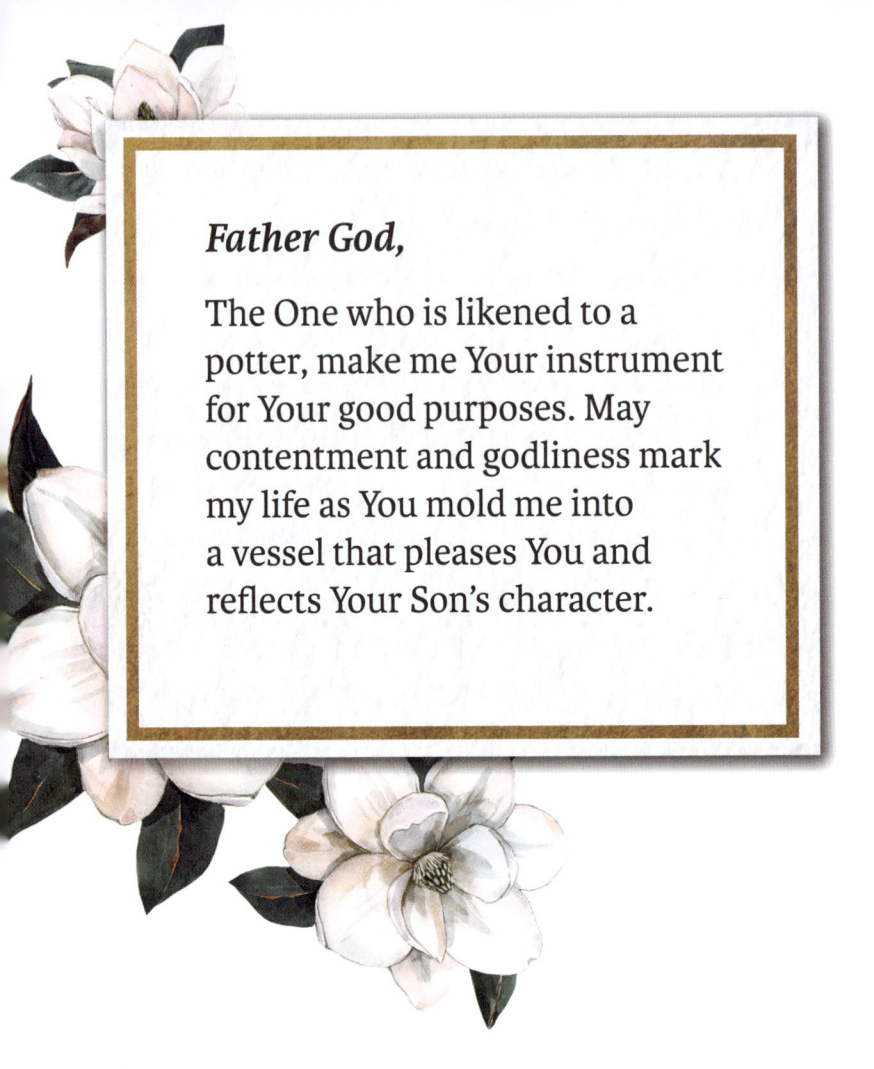

The One who is likened to a potter, make me Your instrument for Your good purposes. May contentment and godliness mark my life as You mold me into a vessel that pleases You and reflects Your Son's character.

But now, O Yahweh, You are our Father; we are the clay, and You our potter; and all of us are the work of Your hand.

ISAIAH 64:8

Lord,

Please hear my cries regarding my loved ones. I care deeply about each one of them. I know I can bring them before You in prayer and that You are at work in their lives. Although I can't see everything, I know You are with them. Thank You for hearing my prayers.

Now to Him who is able to do far more abundantly beyond all that we ask or understand, according to the power that works within us, to Him be the glory in the church and in Christ Jesus to all generations forever and ever. Amen.

EPHESIANS 3:20-21

Dear Jesus,

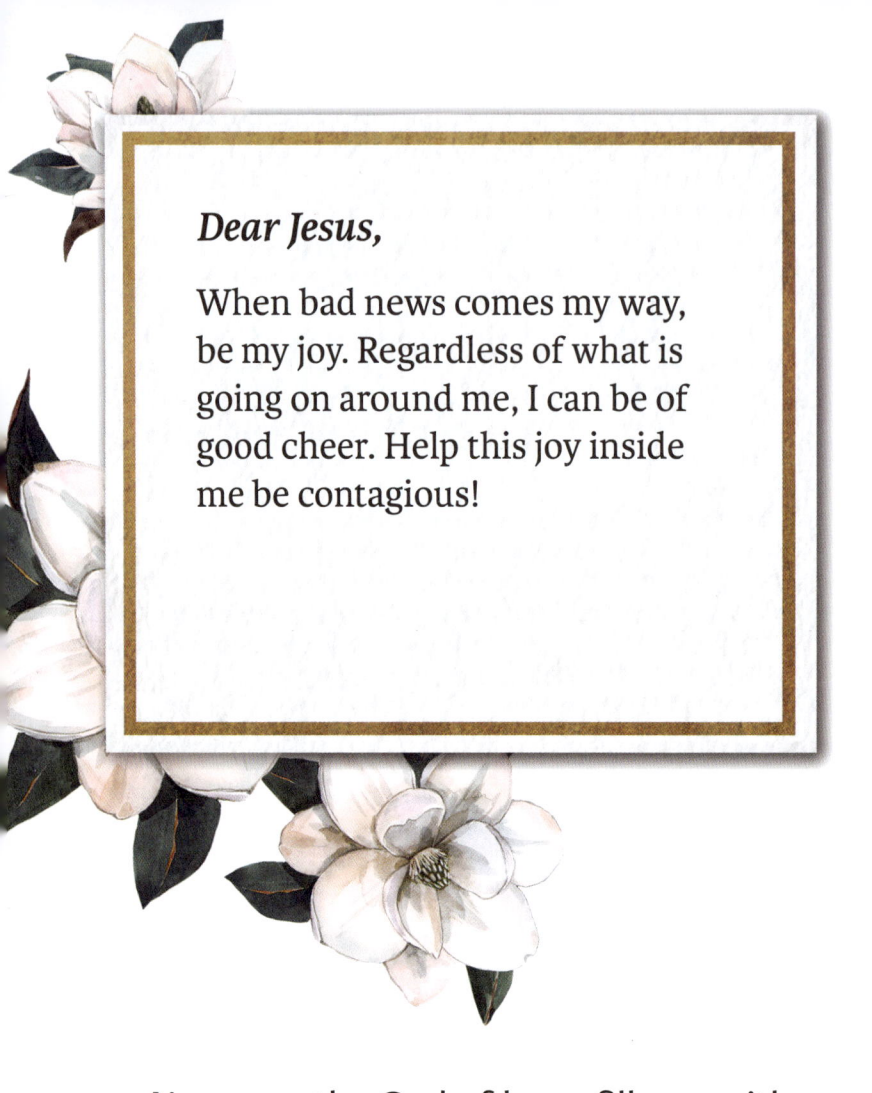

When bad news comes my way, be my joy. Regardless of what is going on around me, I can be of good cheer. Help this joy inside me be contagious!

Now may the God of hope fill you with all joy and peace in believing, so that you will abound in hope by the power of the Holy Spirit.

ROMANS 15:13

Lord,

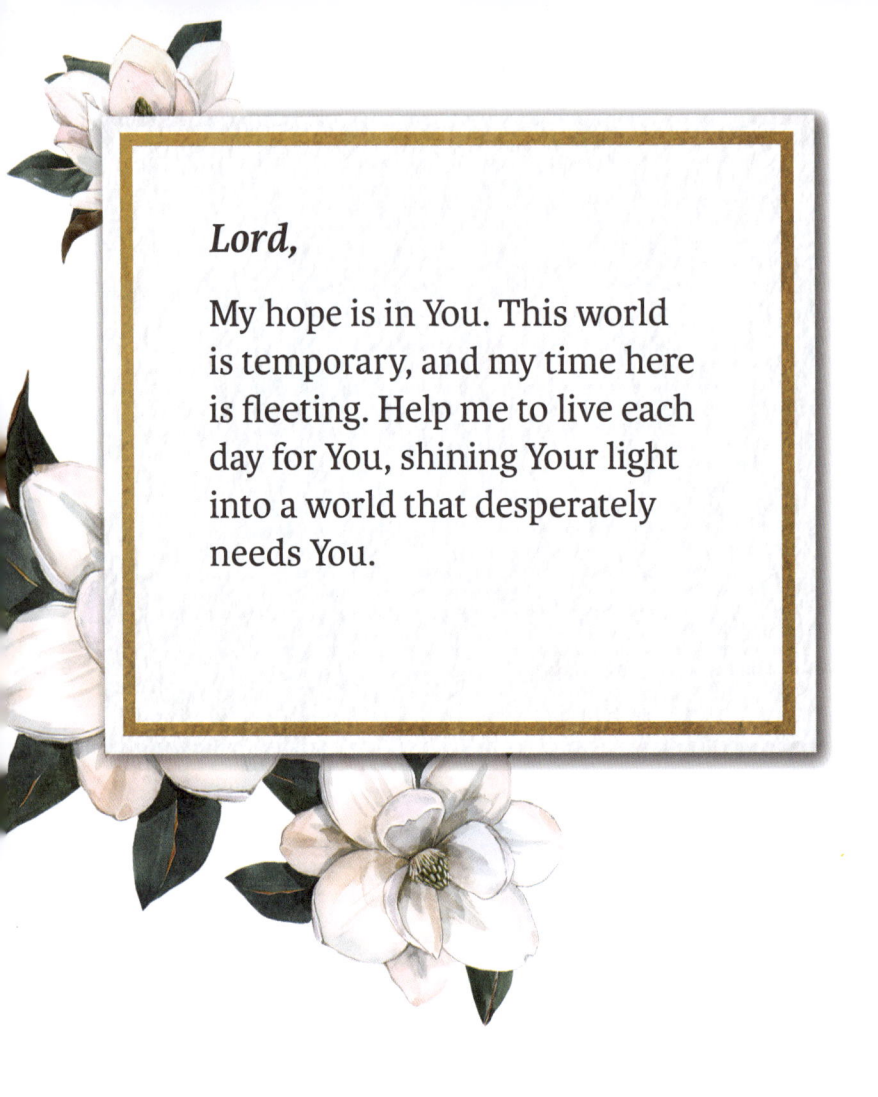

My hope is in You. This world is temporary, and my time here is fleeting. Help me to live each day for You, shining Your light into a world that desperately needs You.

Set your mind on the things above, not on the things that are on earth.

COLOSSIANS 3:2

God,

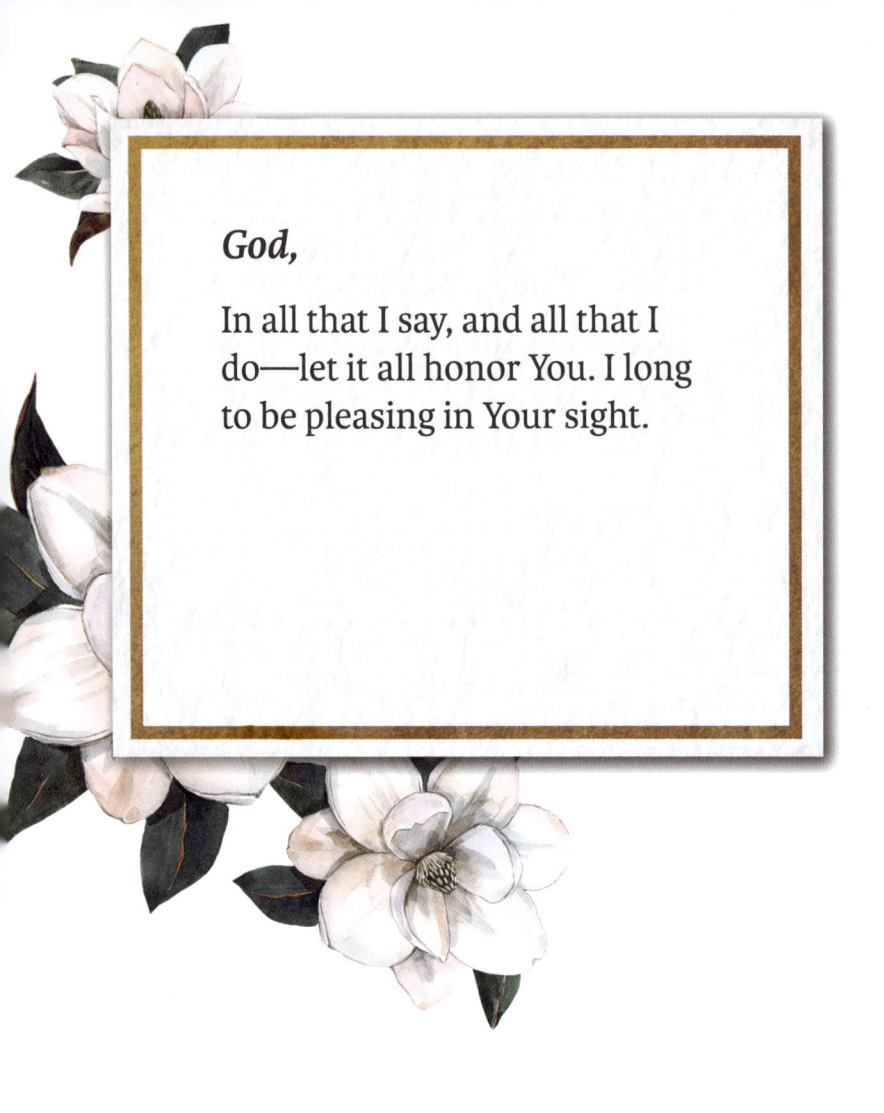

In all that I say, and all that I do—let it all honor You. I long to be pleasing in Your sight.

Whatever you do in word or deed, do all in the name of the Lord Jesus, giving thanks through Him to God the Father.

COLOSSIANS 3:17 NASB

Lord,

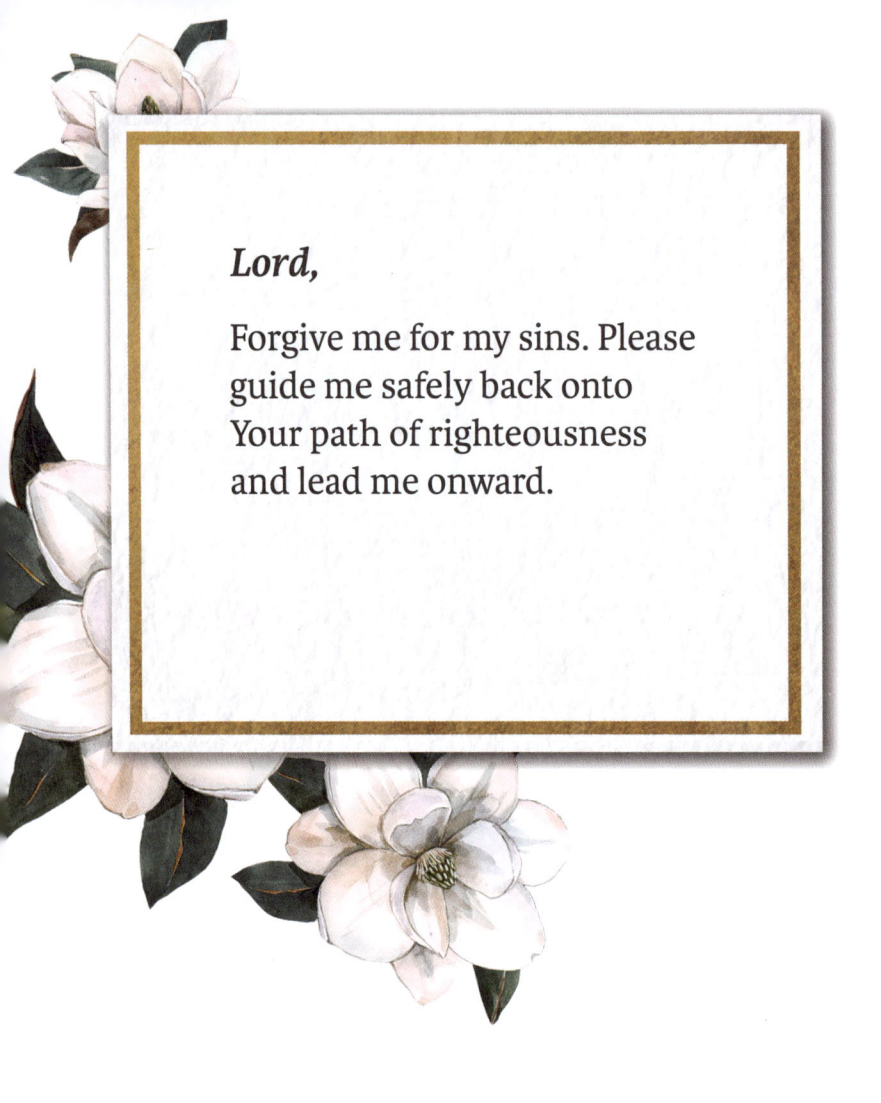

Forgive me for my sins. Please guide me safely back onto Your path of righteousness and lead me onward.

If we confess our sins, He is faithful and righteous to forgive us our sins and to cleanse us from all unrighteousness.

1 JOHN 1:9

Lord Jesus,

The moment I accepted You as my Savior, I joined the race. Would You help me let go of anything weighing me down? Help me run this lifelong journey in Your strength. Thank You, Jesus, for I know You are with me every step of the way.

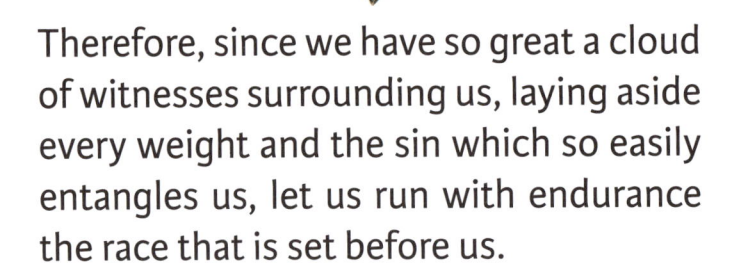

Therefore, since we have so great a cloud of witnesses surrounding us, laying aside every weight and the sin which so easily entangles us, let us run with endurance the race that is set before us.

HEBREWS 12:1

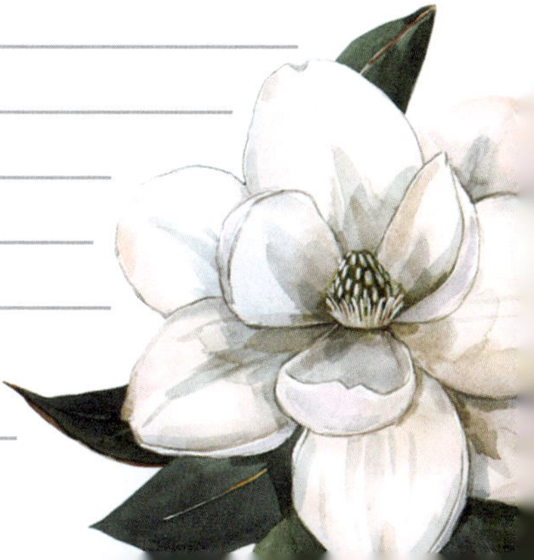

Lord,

All those worries I had at night seem small now, as a new day dawns before me. Thank You for being my constant calming presence.

Be anxious for nothing, but in everything by prayer and petition with thanksgiving let your requests be made known to God. And the peace of God, which surpasses all comprehension, will guard your hearts and your minds in Christ Jesus.

PHILIPPIANS 4:6-7

Lord God,

This life has its hardships. Sometimes I think of heaven, where every relationship among Your children will be made whole. Until then, I'm grateful for Your healing touch right here, right now.

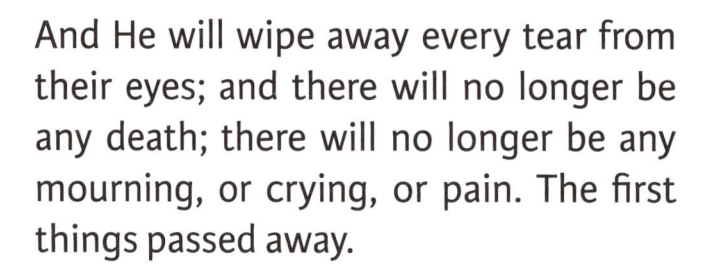

And He will wipe away every tear from their eyes; and there will no longer be any death; there will no longer be any mourning, or crying, or pain. The first things passed away.

REVELATION 21:4

Lord,

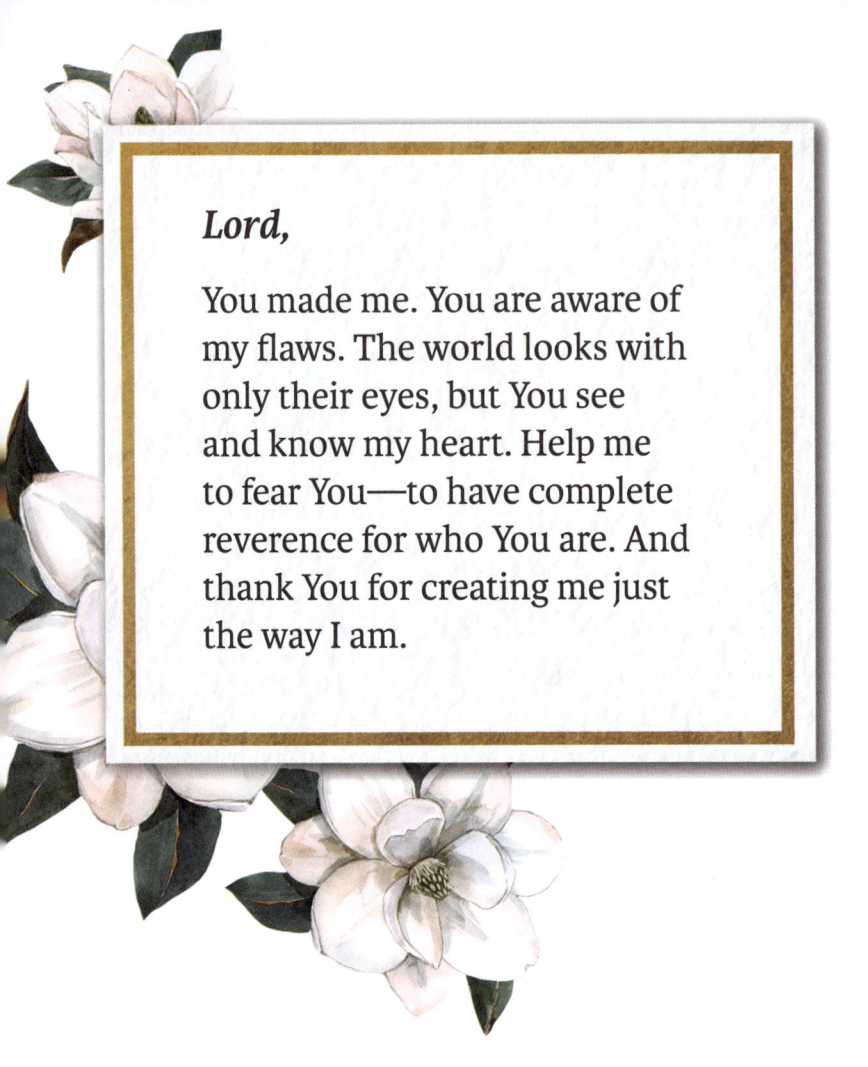

You made me. You are aware of my flaws. The world looks with only their eyes, but You see and know my heart. Help me to fear You—to have complete reverence for who You are. And thank You for creating me just the way I am.

Charm is deceitful and beauty is vain, but a woman who fears the LORD, she shall be praised.

PROVERBS 31:30 NASB

Almighty God,

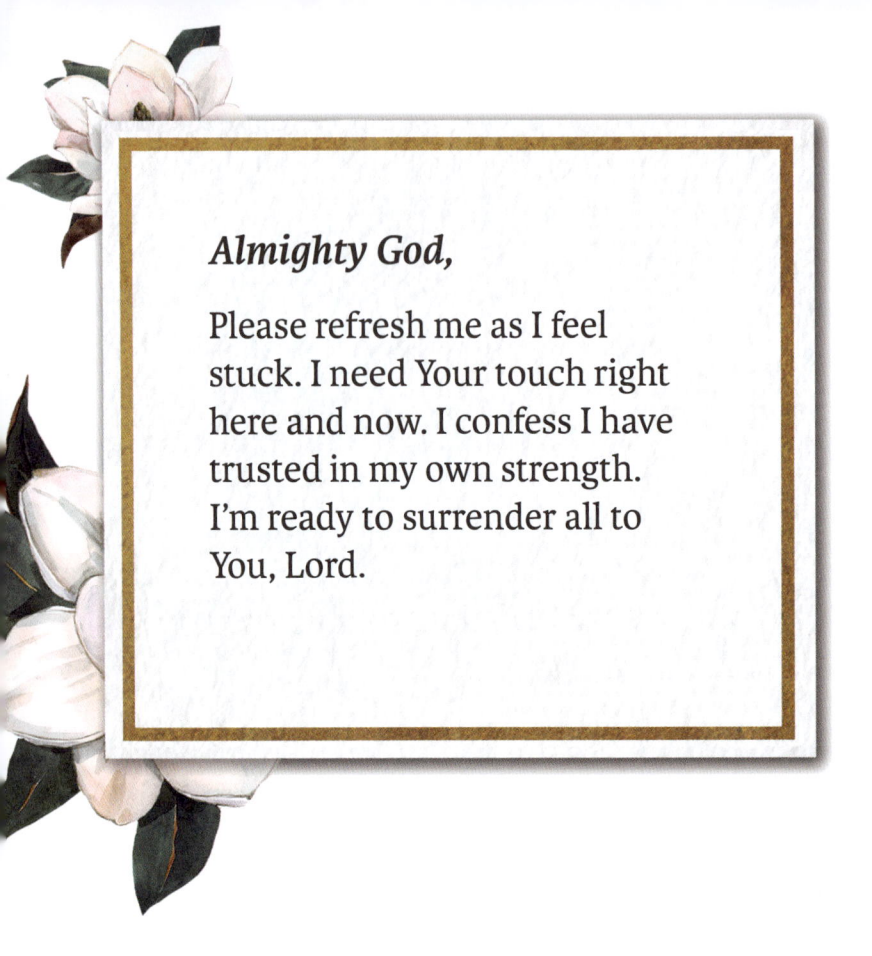

Please refresh me as I feel stuck. I need Your touch right here and now. I confess I have trusted in my own strength. I'm ready to surrender all to You, Lord.

I waited patiently for the LORD; and He inclined to me and heard my cry. He brought me up out of the pit of destruction, out of the miry clay, and He set my feet upon a rock making my footsteps firm.

PSALM 40:1-2 NASB

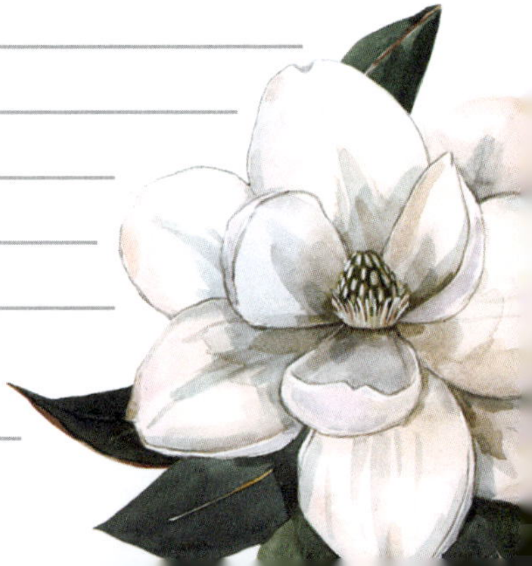

Lord God,

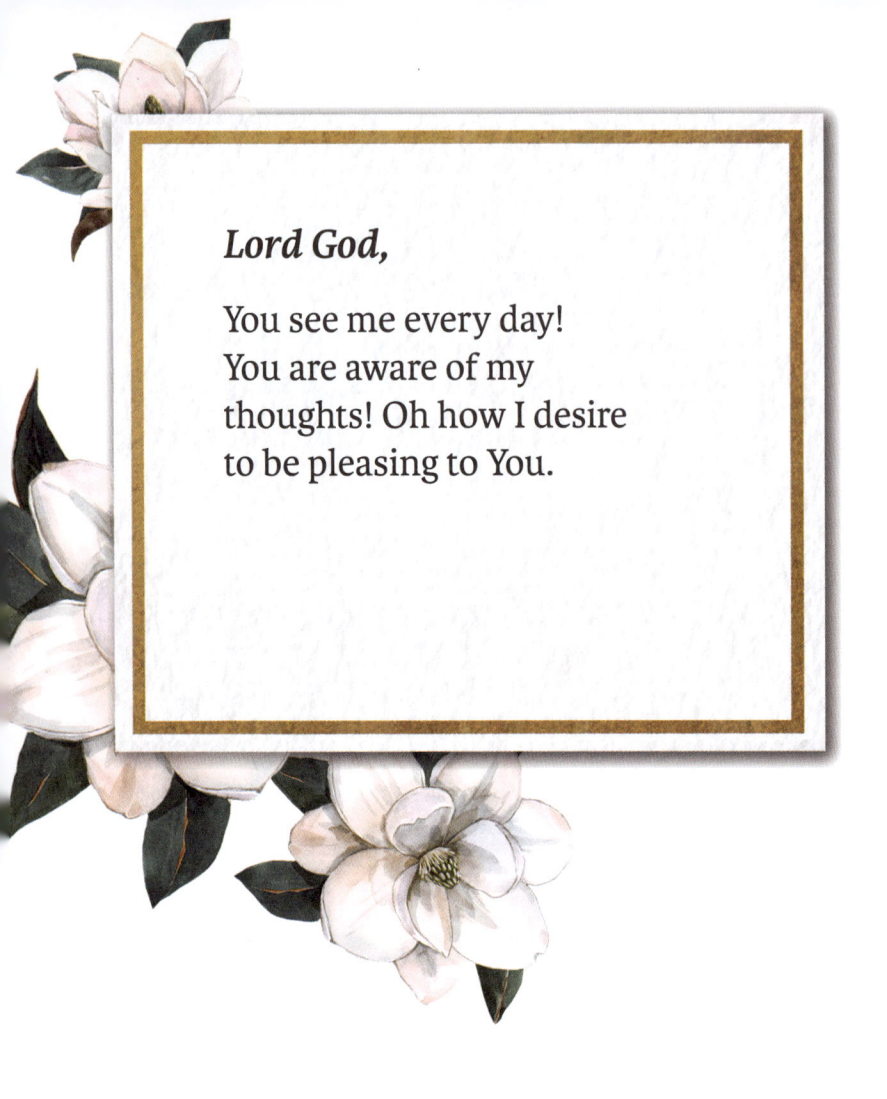

You see me every day! You are aware of my thoughts! Oh how I desire to be pleasing to You.

You know when I sit down and when I rise up; You understand my thought from afar.

PSALM 139:2

Lord,

When there is suffering, help me be a conduit of Your comfort. There is no comfort like the comfort You bring. O Lord, people are hurting. I pray You pour Your mercy upon them.

Blessed be the God and Father of our Lord Jesus Christ, the Father of mercies and God of all comfort, who comforts us in all our affliction so that we will be able to comfort those who are in any affliction with the comfort with which we ourselves are comforted by God.

2 CORINTHIANS 1:3-4

Lord,

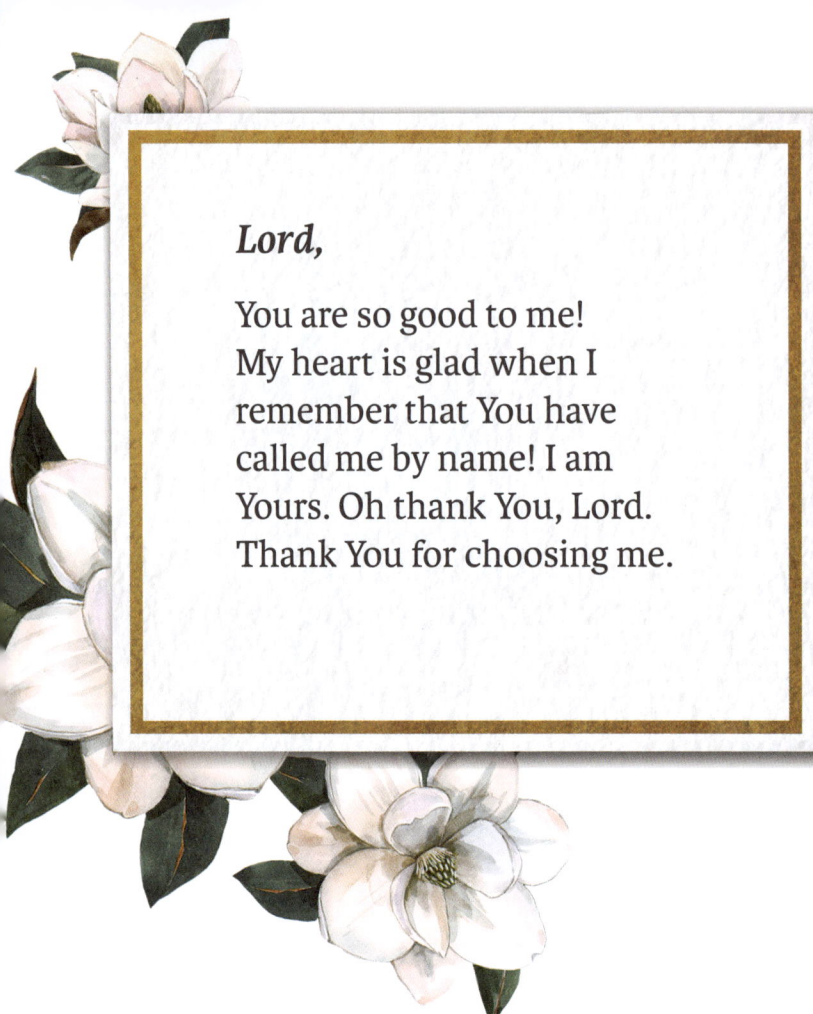

You are so good to me! My heart is glad when I remember that You have called me by name! I am Yours. Oh thank You, Lord. Thank You for choosing me.

But now, thus says the LORD, your Creator, O Jacob, and He who formed you, O Israel, "Do not fear, for I have redeemed you; I have called you by name; you are Mine!"

ISAIAH 43:1 NASB

Dear Jesus,

This world can be overwhelming at times, even scary. Yet, here I am, in this place and time in history. Help me to walk with You, trust in You, and shine for You.

Do not fear, for I am with you; do not anxiously look about you, for I am your God. I will make you mighty, surely I will help you; surely I will uphold you with My righteous right hand.

ISAIAH 41:10

Lord God,

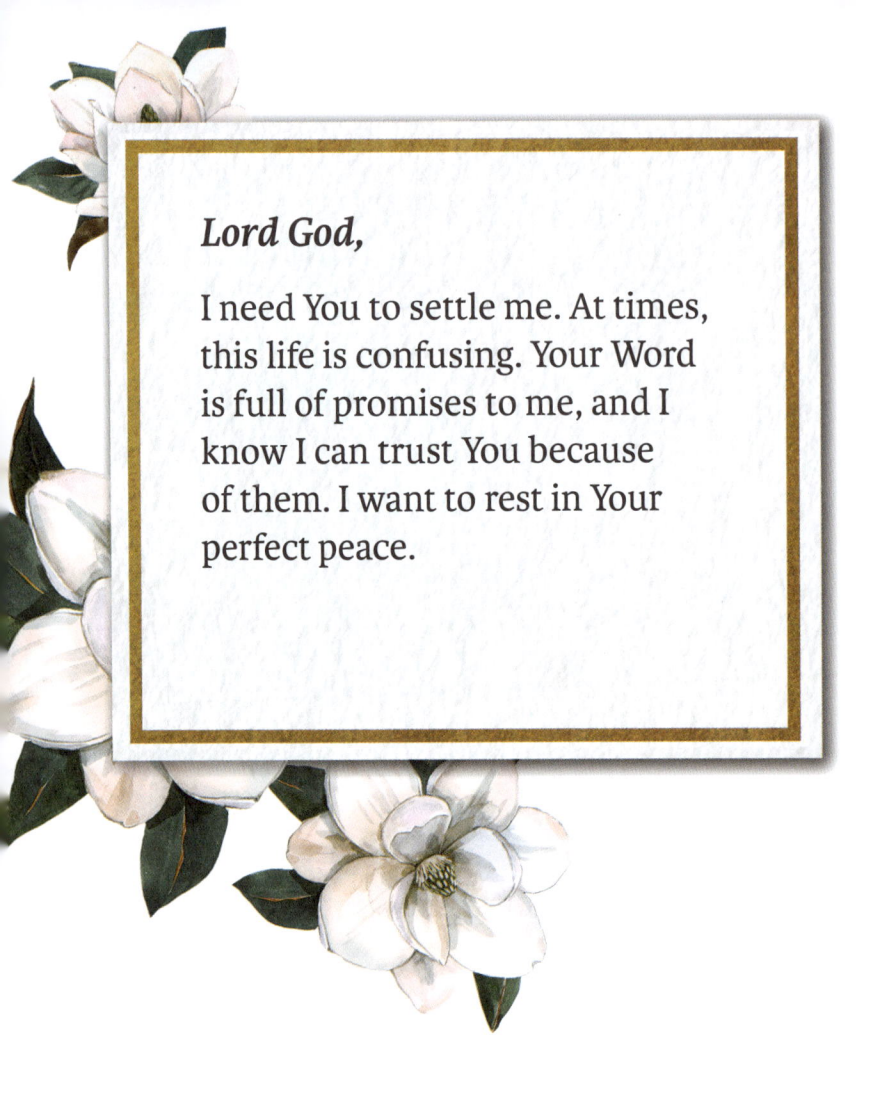

I need You to settle me. At times, this life is confusing. Your Word is full of promises to me, and I know I can trust You because of them. I want to rest in Your perfect peace.

The steadfast of mind You will keep in perfect peace because he trusts in You.

ISAIAH 26:3

Lord,

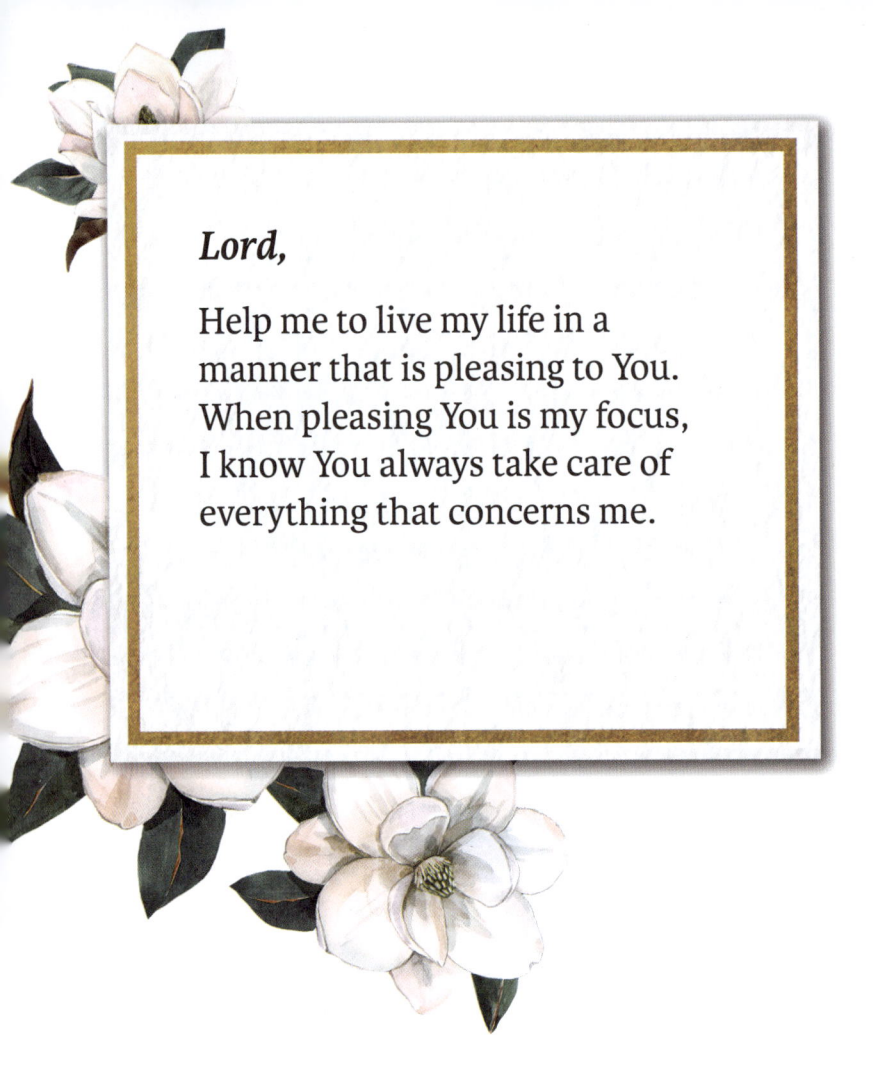

Help me to live my life in a manner that is pleasing to You. When pleasing You is my focus, I know You always take care of everything that concerns me.

This is good and acceptable in the sight of God our Savior, who desires all men to be saved and to come to the full knowledge of the truth.

1 TIMOTHY 2:3-4

Lord,

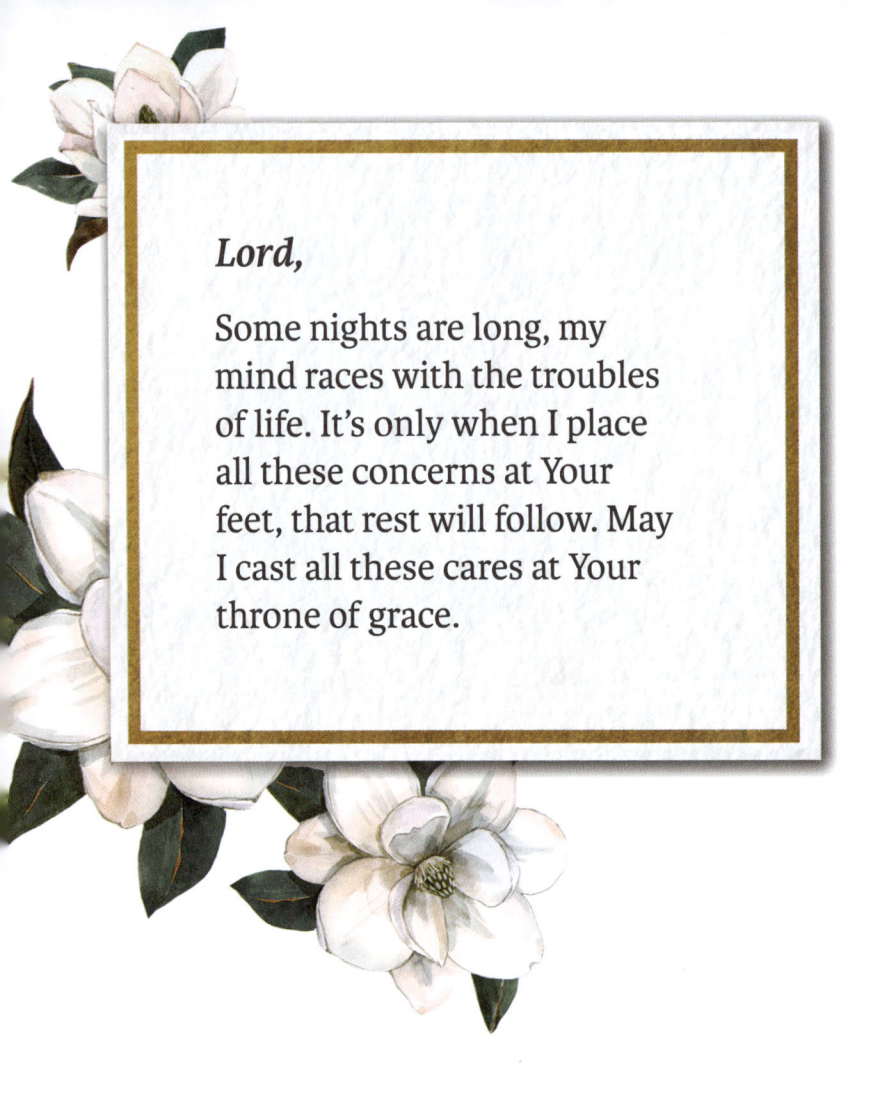

Some nights are long, my mind races with the troubles of life. It's only when I place all these concerns at Your feet, that rest will follow. May I cast all these cares at Your throne of grace.

In peace I will both lie down and sleep, for You alone, O LORD, make me to dwell in safety.

PSALM 4:8 NASB

Lord God,

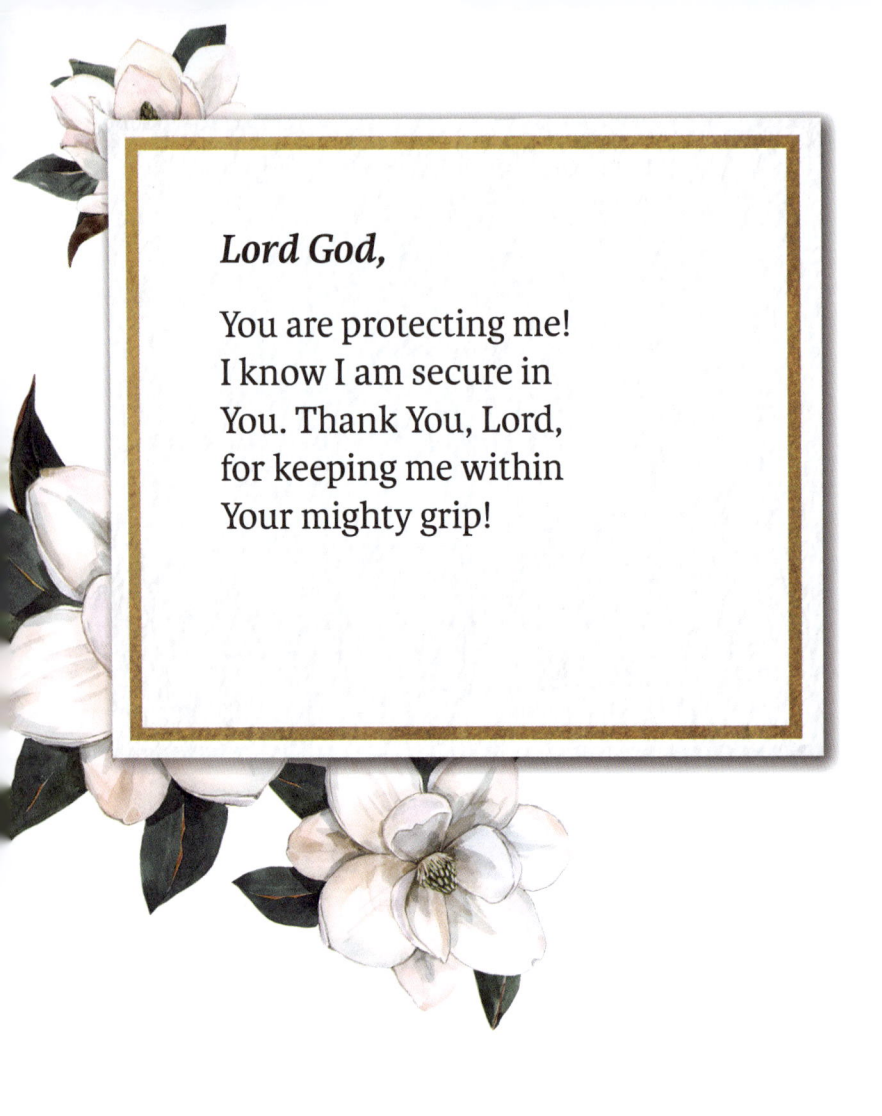

You are protecting me! I know I am secure in You. Thank You, Lord, for keeping me within Your mighty grip!

You have enclosed me behind and before, and You have put Your hand upon me.

PSALM 139:5

Oh, Lord God!

My problems overwhelm me! There are days when I feel like throwing in the towel. But, when I compare my temporary problem with Your infinite power, I find comfort just knowing the God of the universe cares about me. This trial will pass, but You, Lord, are unchanging.

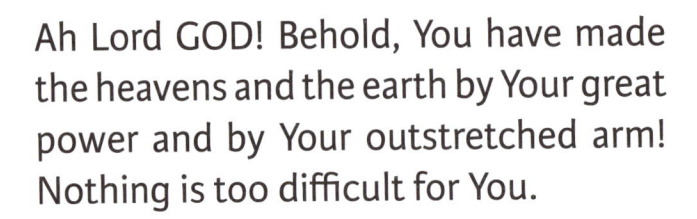

Ah Lord GOD! Behold, You have made the heavens and the earth by Your great power and by Your outstretched arm! Nothing is too difficult for You.

JEREMIAH 32:17 NASB

Lord,

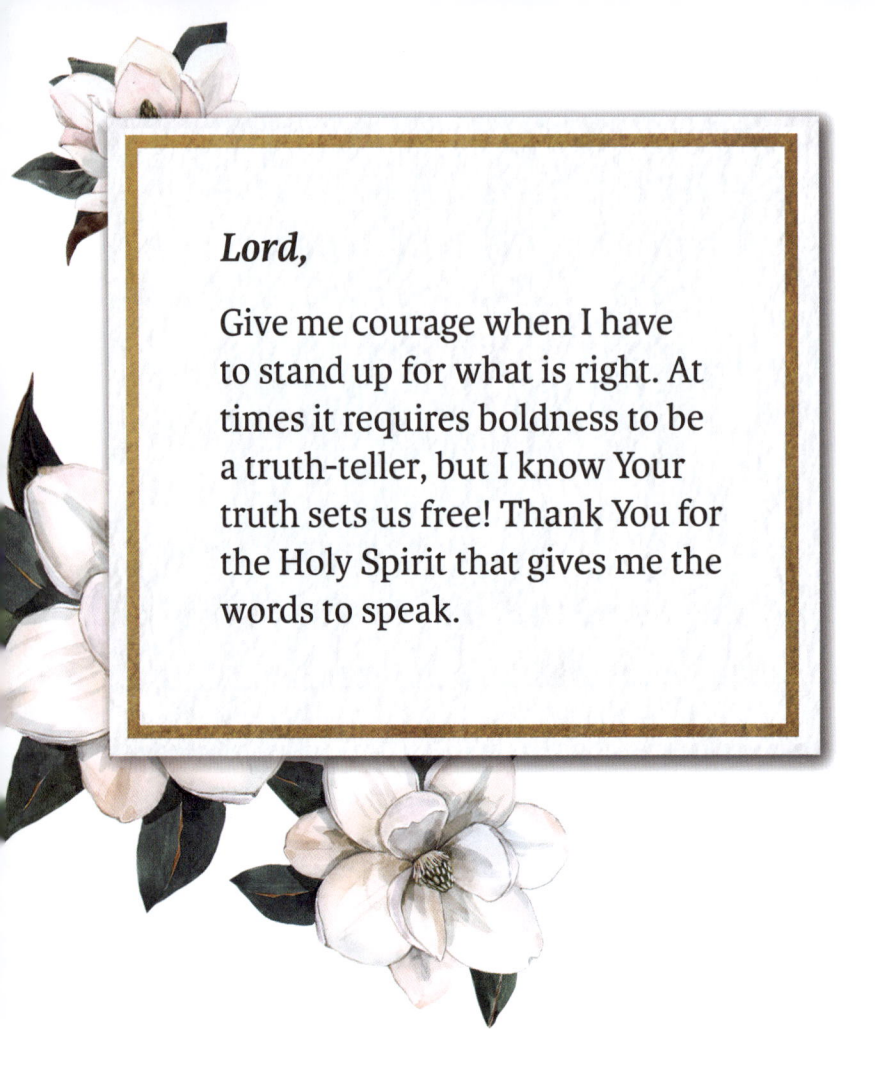

Give me courage when I have to stand up for what is right. At times it requires boldness to be a truth-teller, but I know Your truth sets us free! Thank You for the Holy Spirit that gives me the words to speak.

If you abide in My word, then you are truly My disciples; and you will know the truth, and the truth will make you free.

JOHN 8:31b-32

Lord,

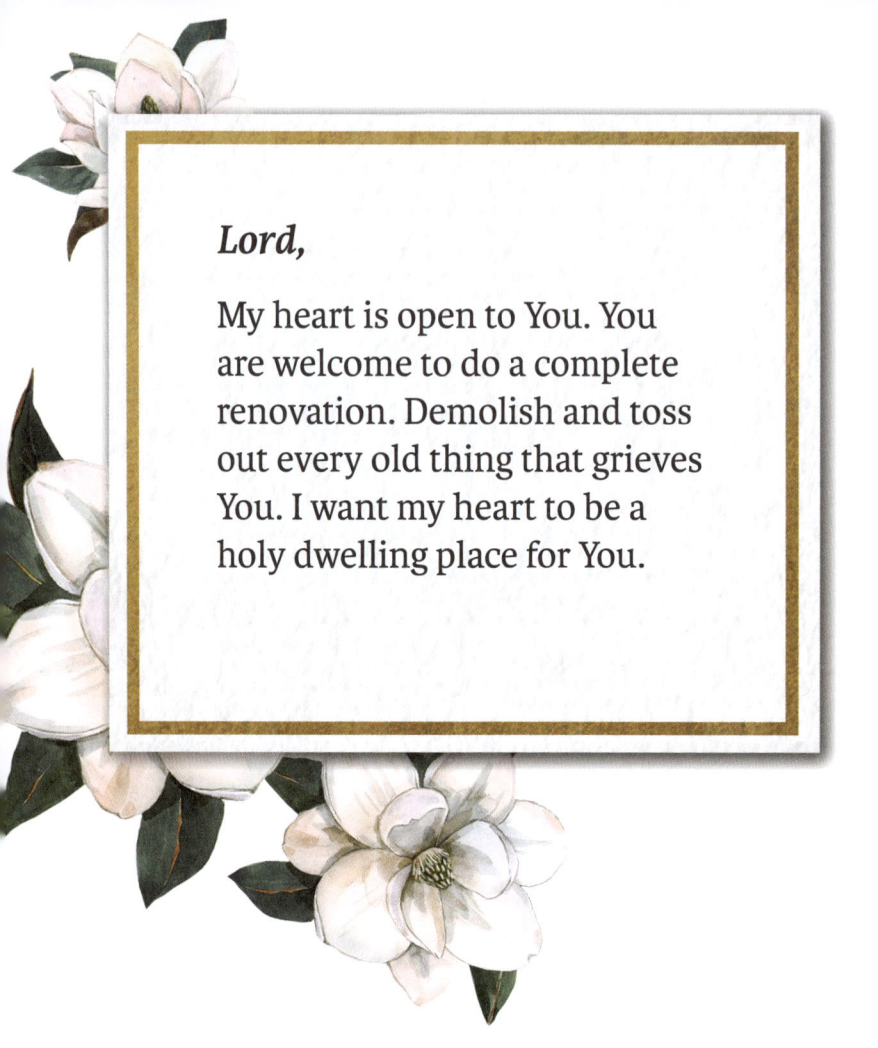

My heart is open to You. You are welcome to do a complete renovation. Demolish and toss out every old thing that grieves You. I want my heart to be a holy dwelling place for You.

Moreover, I will give you a new heart and put a new spirit within you; and I will remove the heart of stone from your flesh and give you a heart of flesh.

EZEKIEL 36:26

Thank You, Lord,

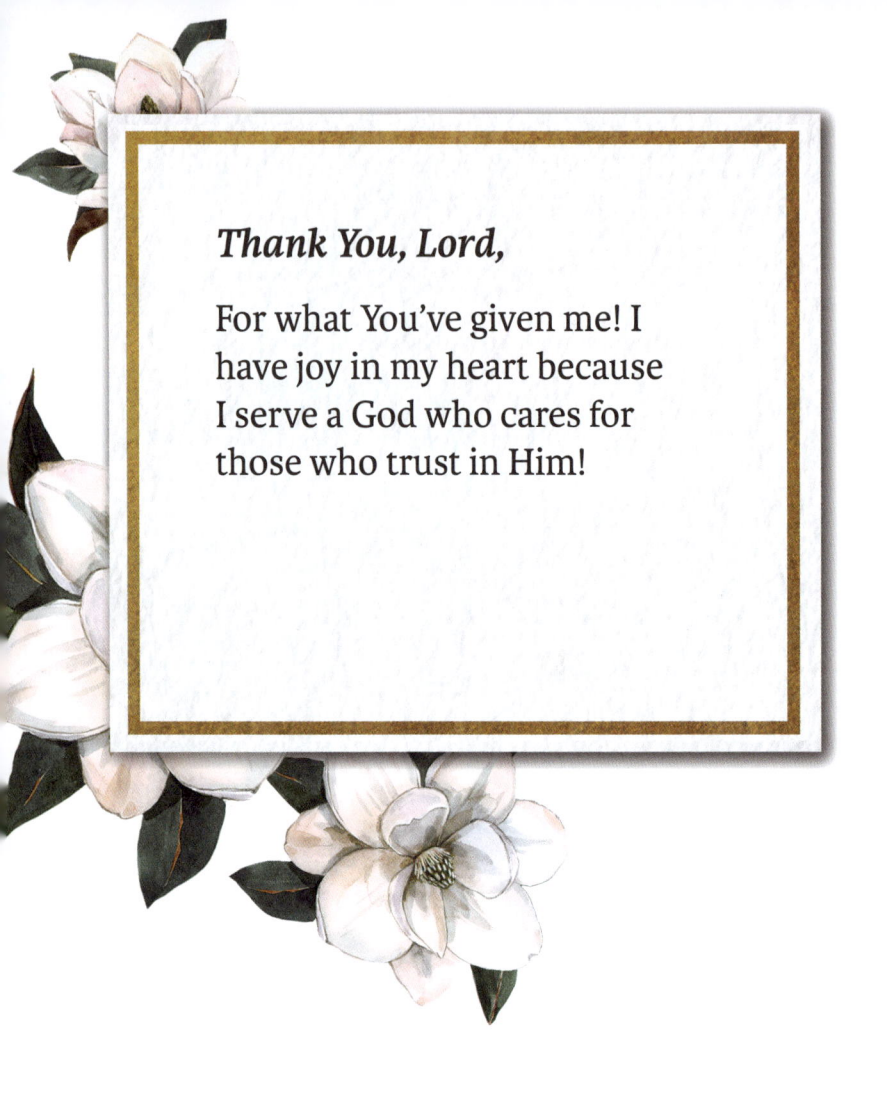

For what You've given me! I have joy in my heart because I serve a God who cares for those who trust in Him!

O taste and see that the LORD is good; how blessed is the man who takes refuge in Him!

PSALM 34:8 NASB

Lord Jesus,

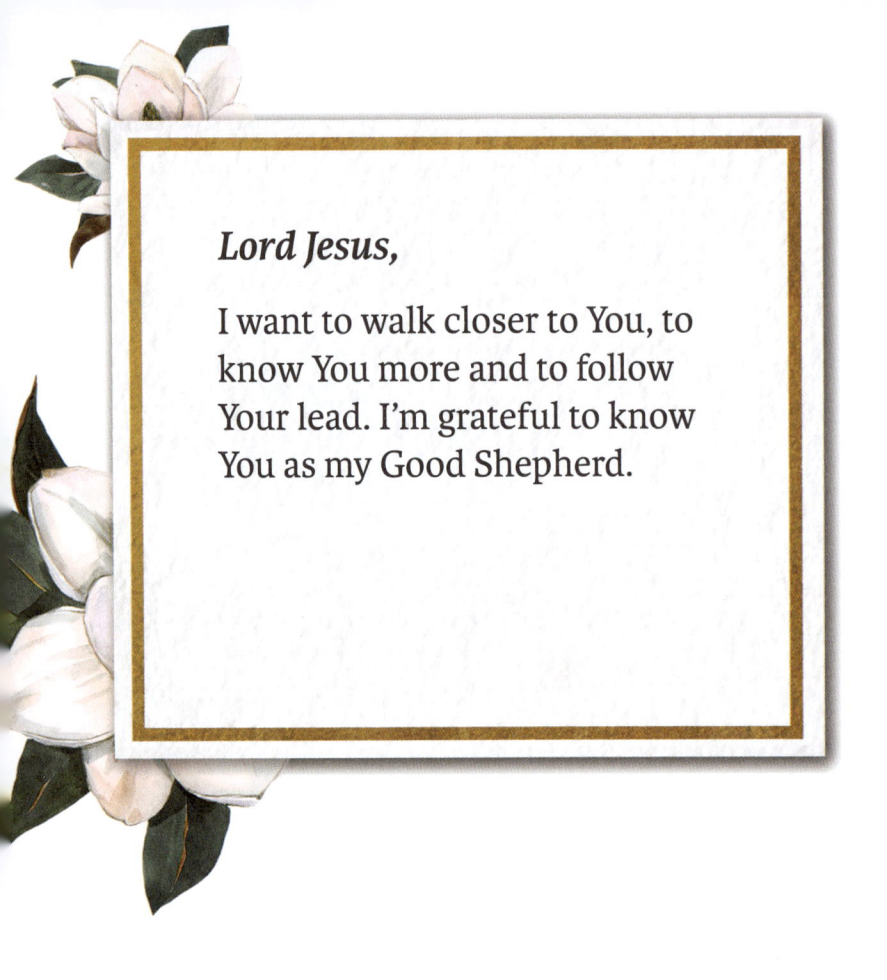

I want to walk closer to You, to know You more and to follow Your lead. I'm grateful to know You as my Good Shepherd.

More than that, I count all things to be loss because of the surpassing value of knowing Christ Jesus my Lord, for whom I have suffered the loss of all things, and count them but rubbish so that I may gain Christ.

PHILIPPIANS 3:8

Lord,

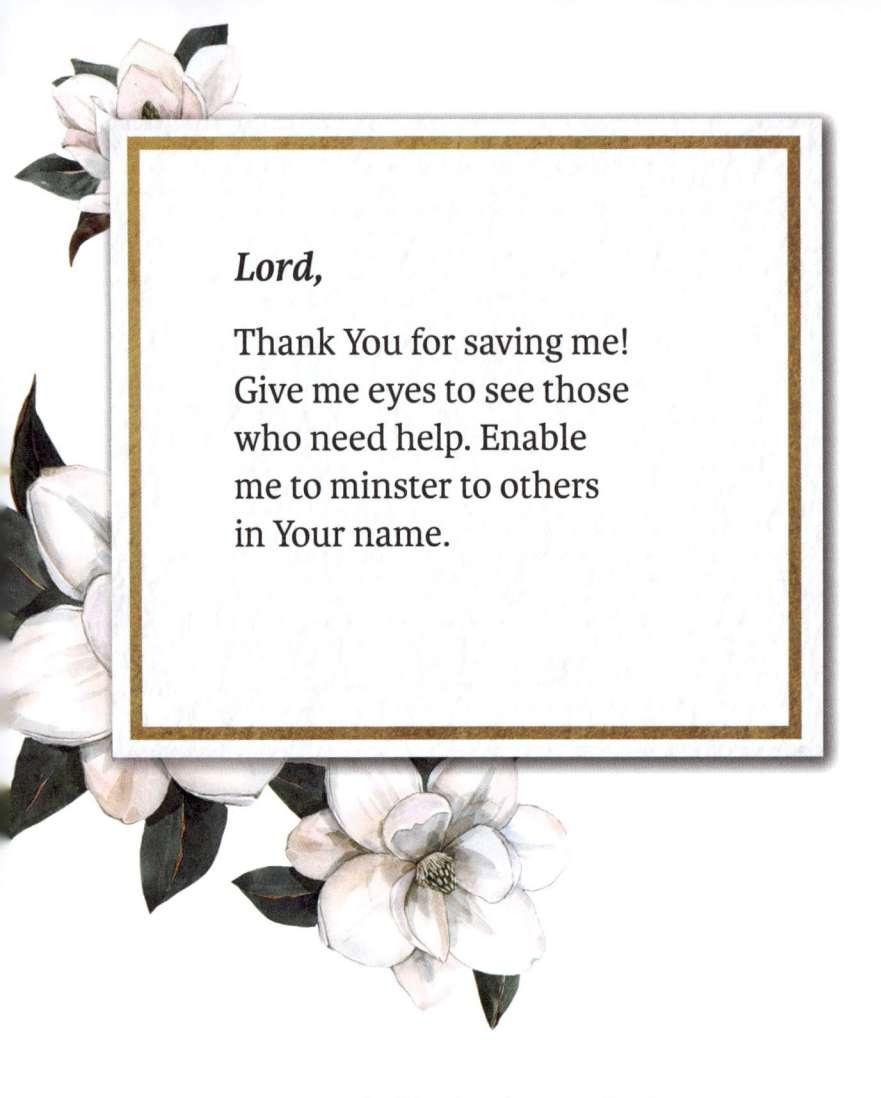

Thank You for saving me! Give me eyes to see those who need help. Enable me to minster to others in Your name.

Pure and undefiled religion before our God and Father is this: to visit orphans and widows in their affliction, and to keep oneself unstained by the world.

JAMES 1:27

Father God,

You pour out abundant blessings into my life; so many of them that the list I thank You for is far too short and incomplete. Today I want to count Your blessings, one by one. Please expand my awareness of Your goodness toward me, that I might grow in my gratitude for Your bountiful grace.

God, our God, blesses us.

PSALM 67:6b

Jesus,

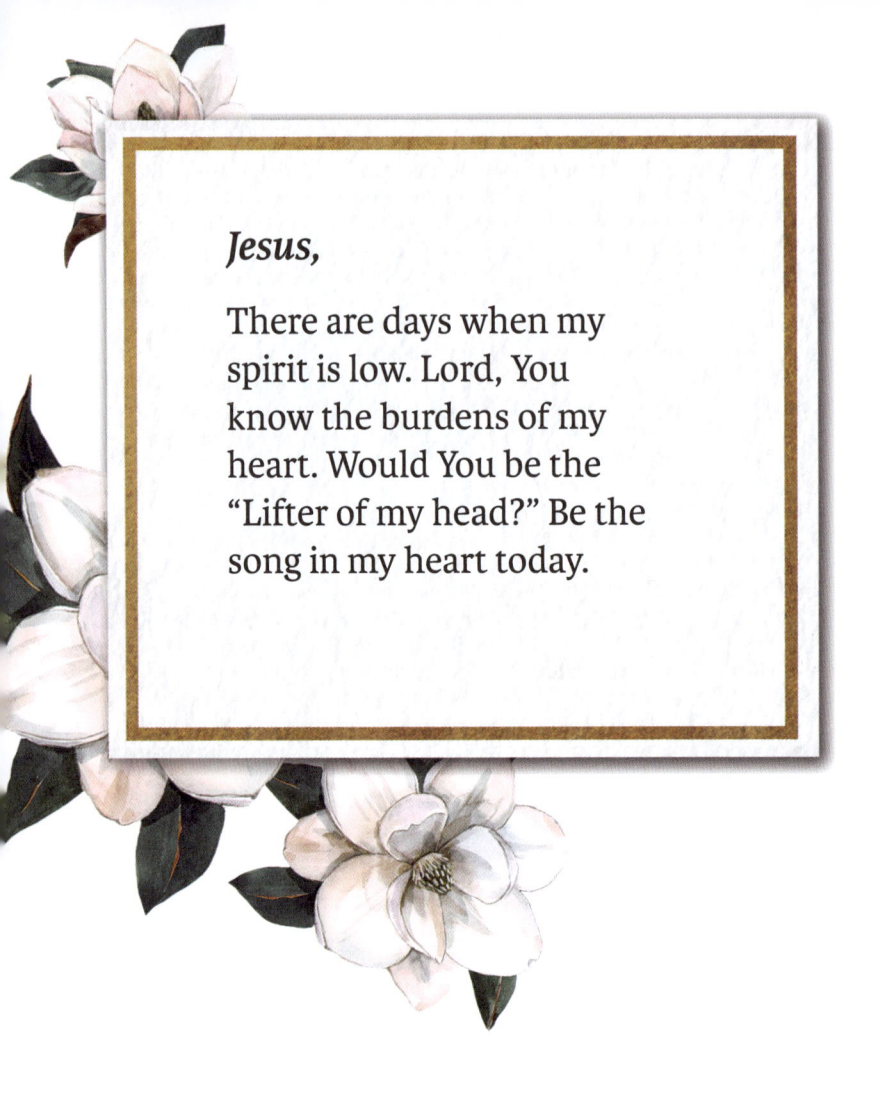

There are days when my spirit is low. Lord, You know the burdens of my heart. Would You be the "Lifter of my head?" Be the song in my heart today.

Is anyone among you suffering? Then he must pray. Is anyone cheerful? He is to sing praises.

JAMES 5:13

O Lord,

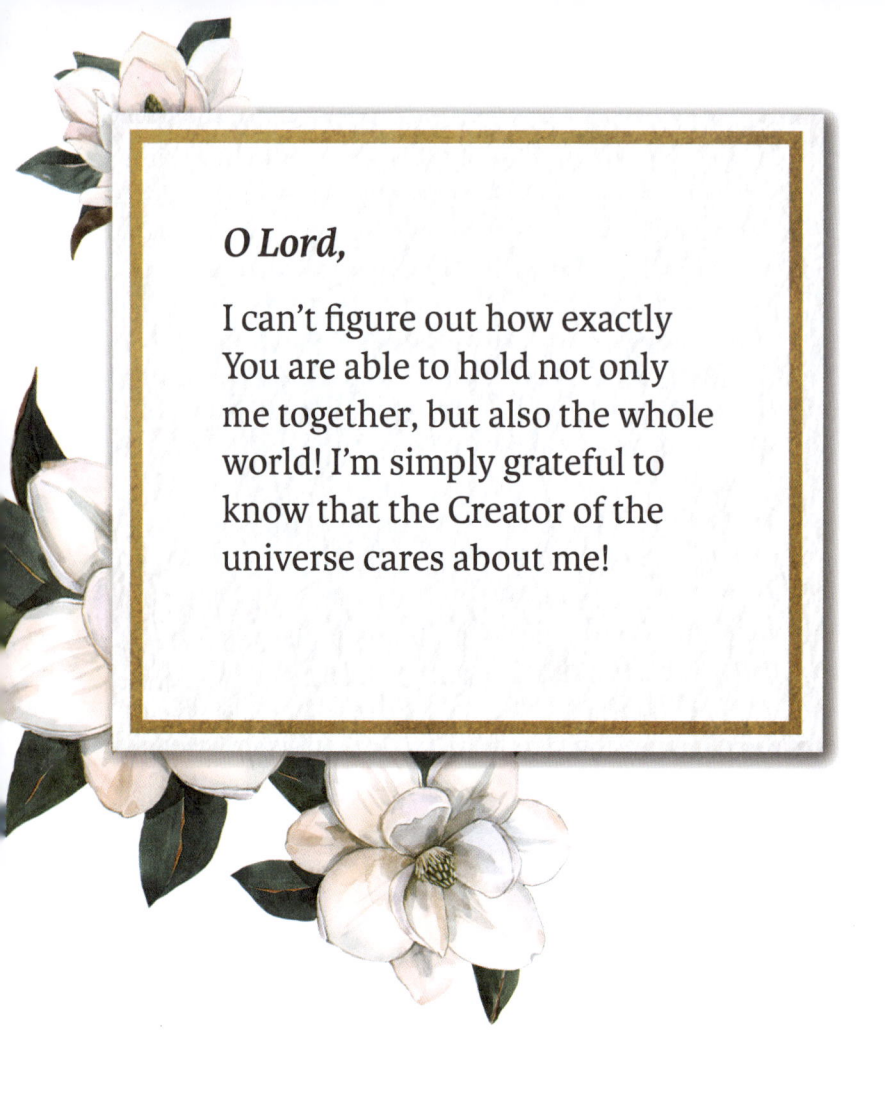

I can't figure out how exactly You are able to hold not only me together, but also the whole world! I'm simply grateful to know that the Creator of the universe cares about me!

Such knowledge is too wonderful for me; it is too high, I cannot attain to it.

PSALM 139:6

Lord Jesus,

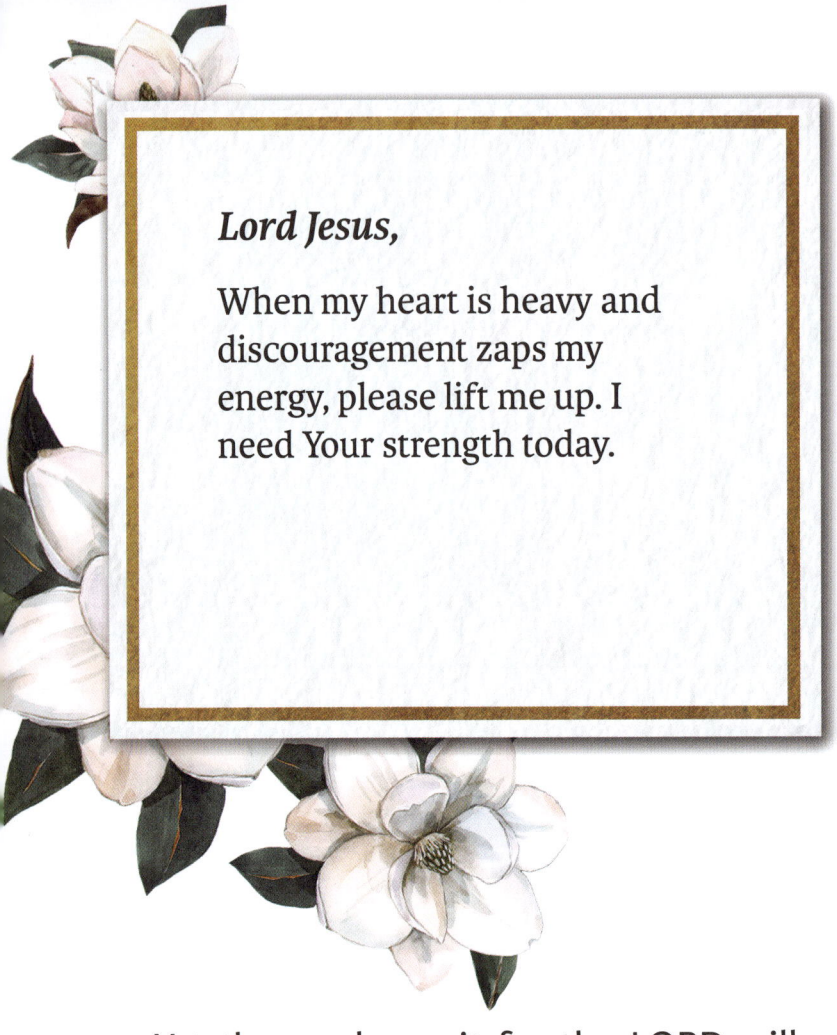

When my heart is heavy and discouragement zaps my energy, please lift me up. I need Your strength today.

Yet those who wait for the LORD will gain new strength; they will mount up with wings like eagles, they will run and not get tired, they will walk and not become weary.

ISAIAH 40:31 NASB

O God,

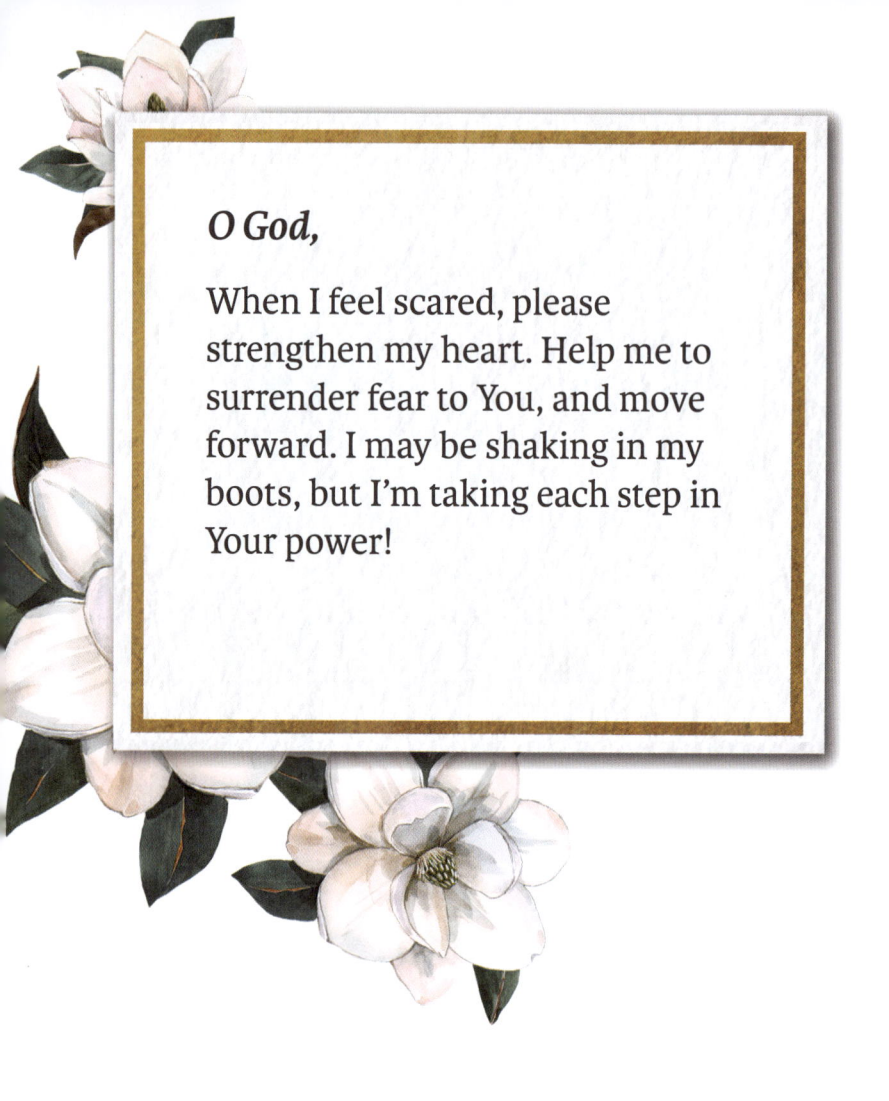

When I feel scared, please strengthen my heart. Help me to surrender fear to You, and move forward. I may be shaking in my boots, but I'm taking each step in Your power!

For God has not given us a spirit of timidity, but of power and love and self-discipline.

2 TIMOTHY 1:7

Lord,

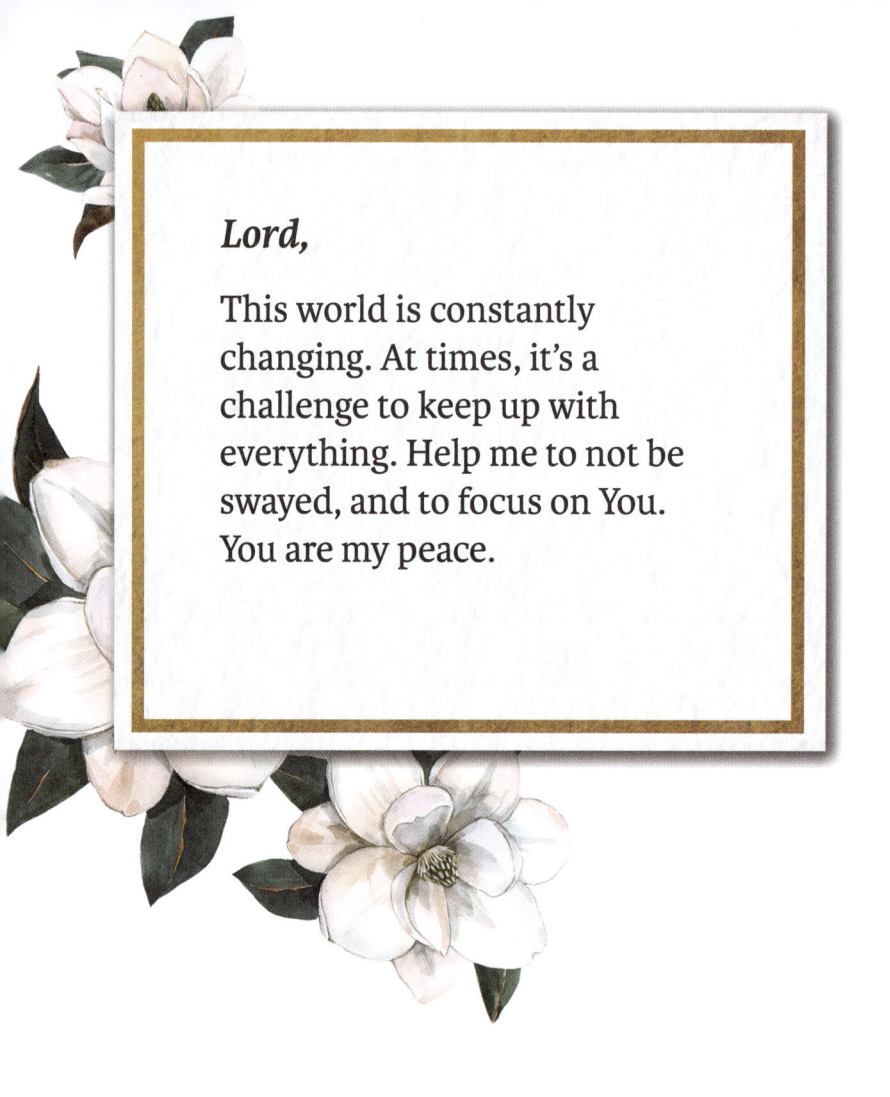

This world is constantly changing. At times, it's a challenge to keep up with everything. Help me to not be swayed, and to focus on You. You are my peace.

Jesus Christ is the same yesterday and today and forever.

HEBREWS 13:8

Lord God,

Help me to remember I can trust in You completely! You know all things, and You care about what concerns me.

This is the confidence which we have before Him, that, if we ask anything according to His will, He hears us.

1 JOHN 5:14 NASB

Lord,

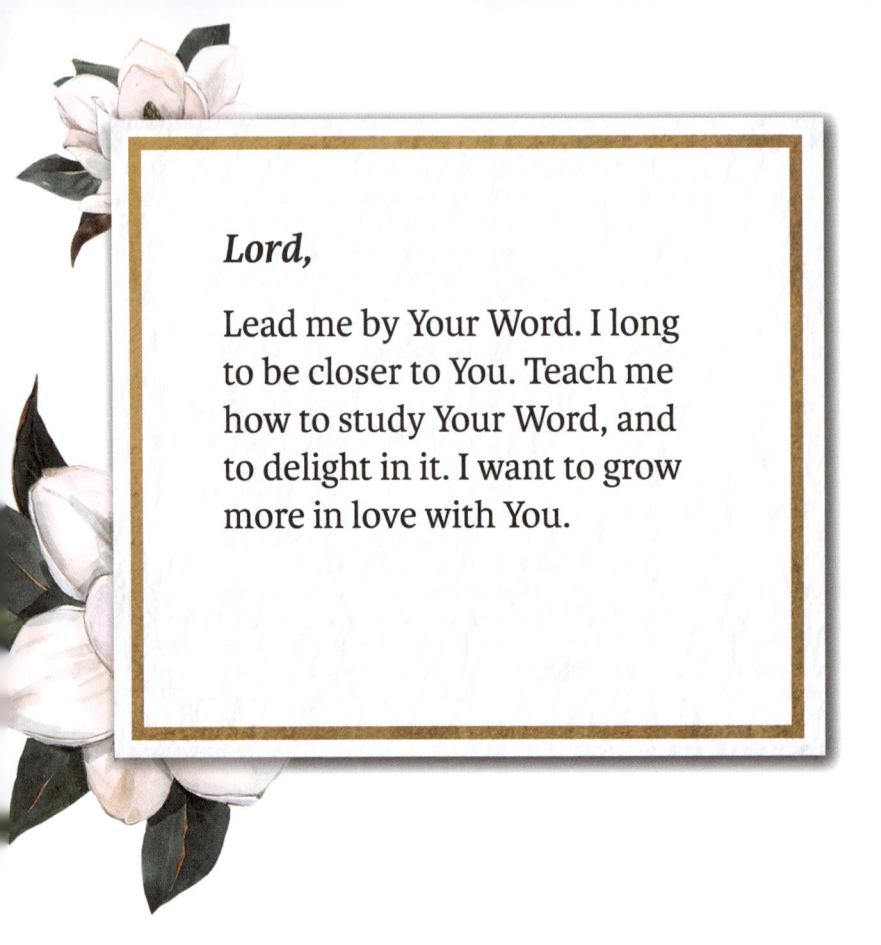

Lead me by Your Word. I long to be closer to You. Teach me how to study Your Word, and to delight in it. I want to grow more in love with You.

But his delight is in the law of the LORD, and in His law he meditates day and night. He will be like a tree firmly planted by streams of water, which yields its fruit in its season and its leaf does not wither; and in whatever he does, he prospers.

PSALM 1:2-3 NASB

Lord,

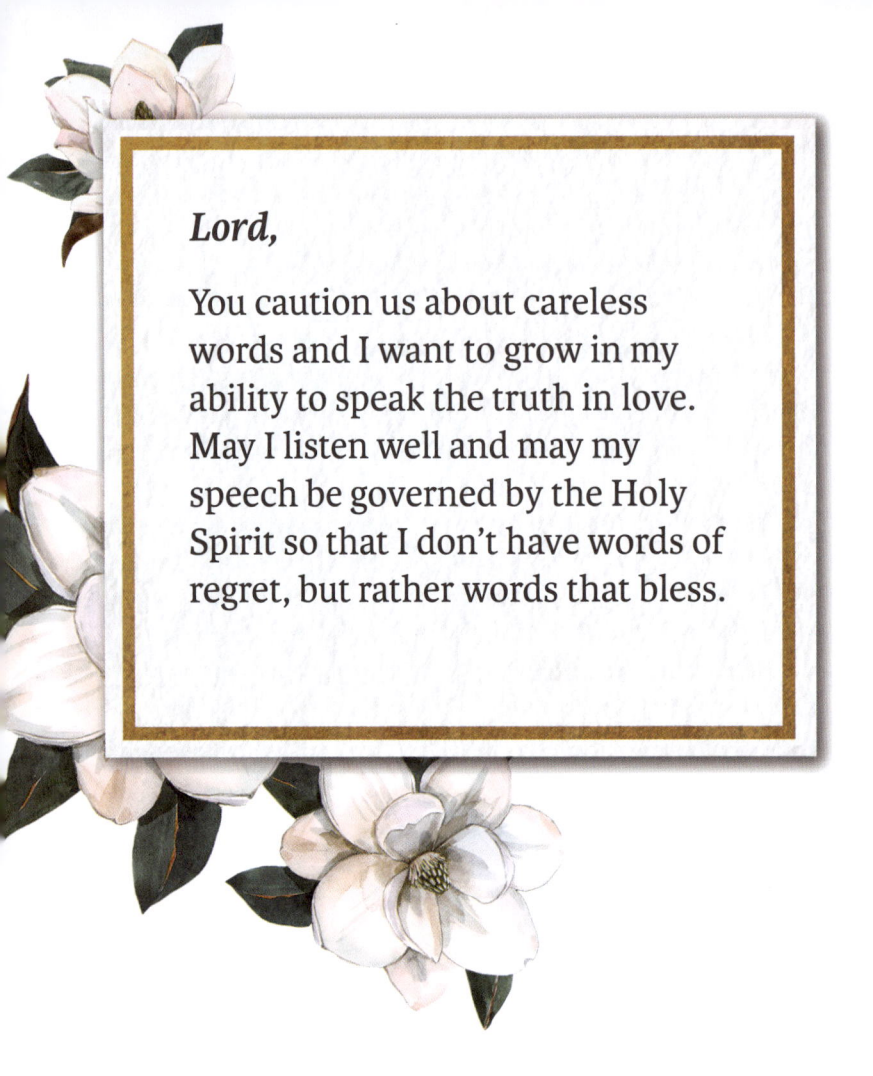

You caution us about careless words and I want to grow in my ability to speak the truth in love. May I listen well and may my speech be governed by the Holy Spirit so that I don't have words of regret, but rather words that bless.

Like apples of gold in settings of silver is a word spoken in right circumstances.

PROVERBS 25:11

Dear Lord,

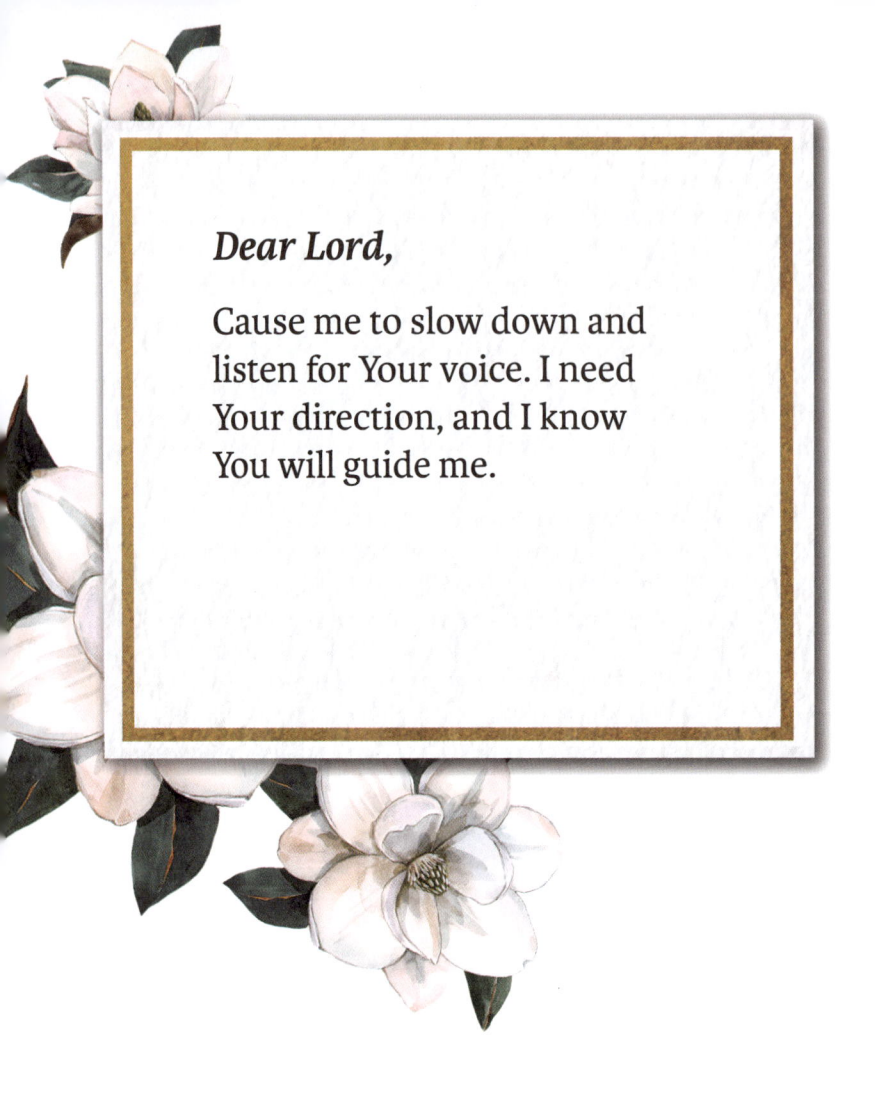

Cause me to slow down and listen for Your voice. I need Your direction, and I know You will guide me.

Lead me in Your truth and teach me, for You are the God of my salvation; in You I hope all the day.

PSALM 25:5

Heavenly Father,

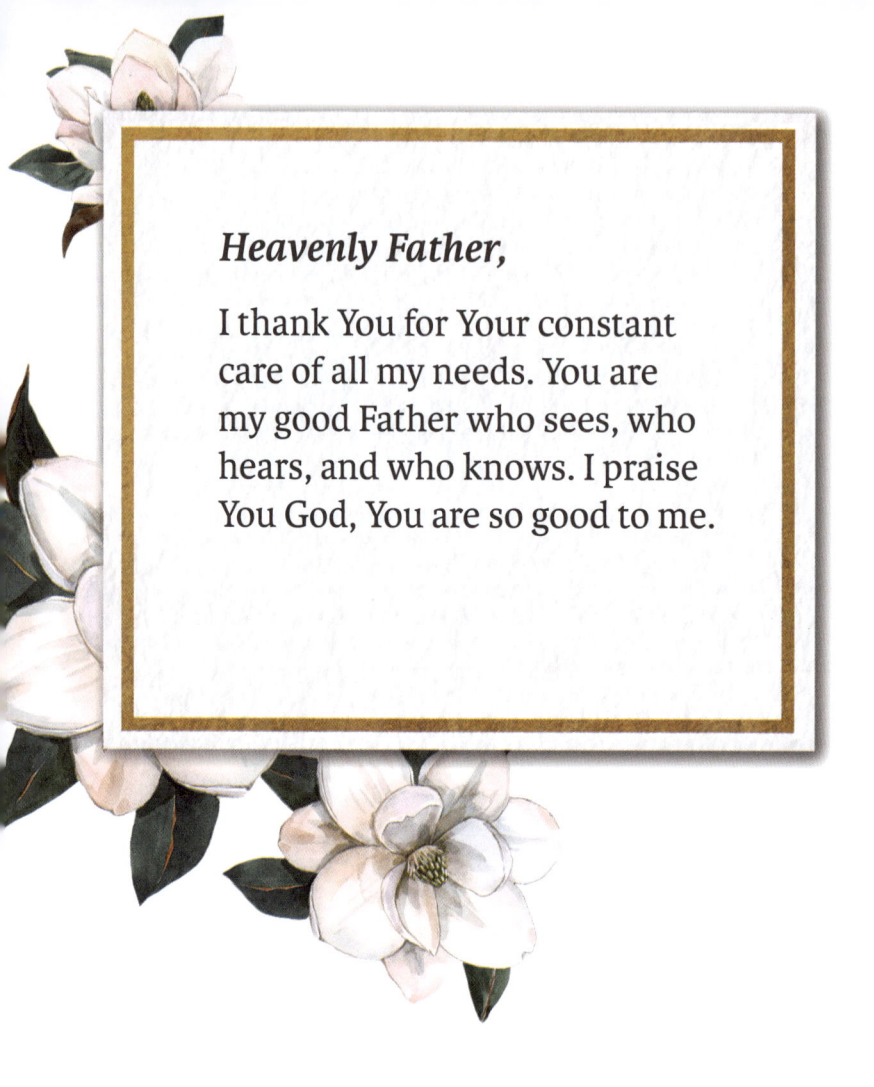

I thank You for Your constant care of all my needs. You are my good Father who sees, who hears, and who knows. I praise You God, You are so good to me.

Just as a father has compassion on his children, so the LORD has compassion on those who fear Him.

PSALM 103:13 NASB

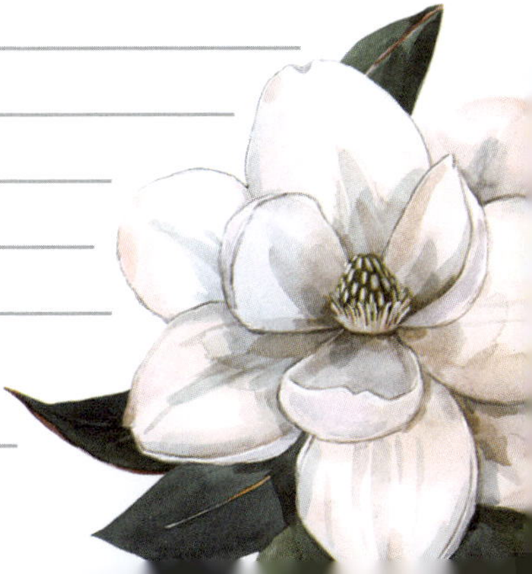

Lord,

Remind me to pray for our leaders more than complain about them. Thank You for those in authority over us. We trust Your perfect plan. Help me to walk according to Your Word, that I may reflect Your light and hope for those who need You.

First of all, then, I exhort that petitions and prayers, requests and thanksgivings, be made for all men, for kings and all who are in authority, so that we may lead a tranquil and quiet life in all godliness and dignity.

1 TIMOTHY 2:1-2

Jesus,

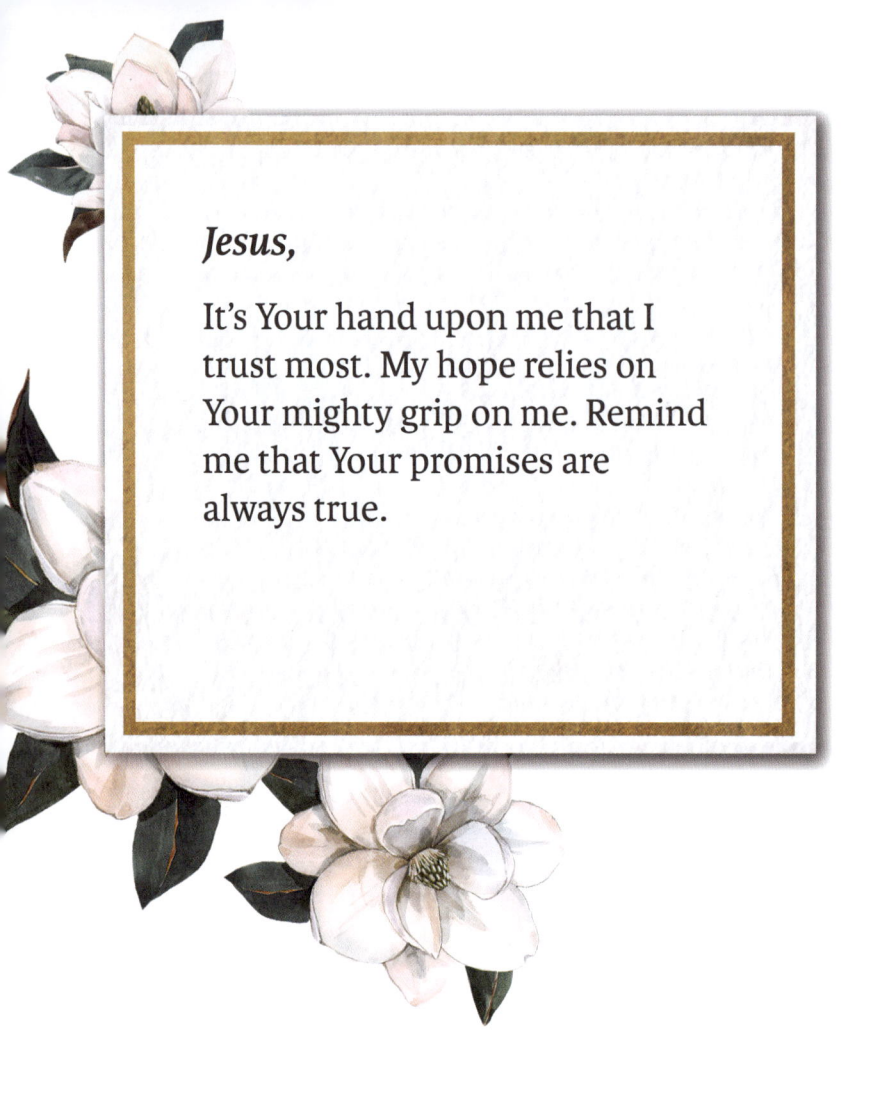

It's Your hand upon me that I trust most. My hope relies on Your mighty grip on me. Remind me that Your promises are always true.

Let us hold fast the confession of our hope without wavering, for He who promised is faithful.

HEBREWS 10:23

Lord,

There are mornings I see the golden colors of the sunrise illuminating all around me. Yet, there are mornings when all I see are gray clouds. But just as I know the sun is shining above, I know You are with me, even when I cannot feel or see You.

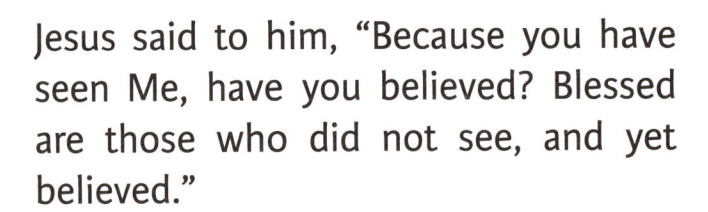

Jesus said to him, "Because you have seen Me, have you believed? Blessed are those who did not see, and yet believed."

JOHN 20:29

Lord God,

I know I can trust You to guide my daily interactions! Thank You for preparing me for whatever comes my way today.

Even before there is a word on my tongue, behold, O Yahweh, You know it all.

PSALM 139:4

Jesus,

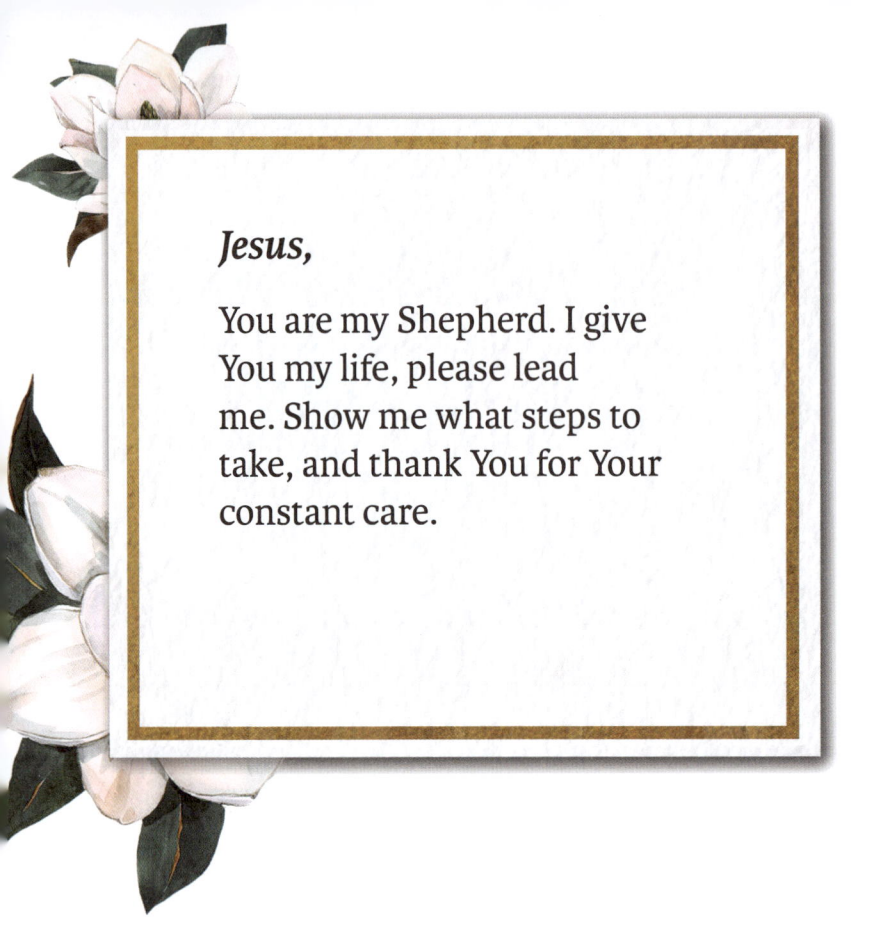

You are my Shepherd. I give You my life, please lead me. Show me what steps to take, and thank You for Your constant care.

To him the doorkeeper opens, and the sheep hear his voice, and he calls his own sheep by name and leads them out. When he brings all his own out, he goes ahead of them, and the sheep follow him because they know his voice.

JOHN 10:3-4

Lord,

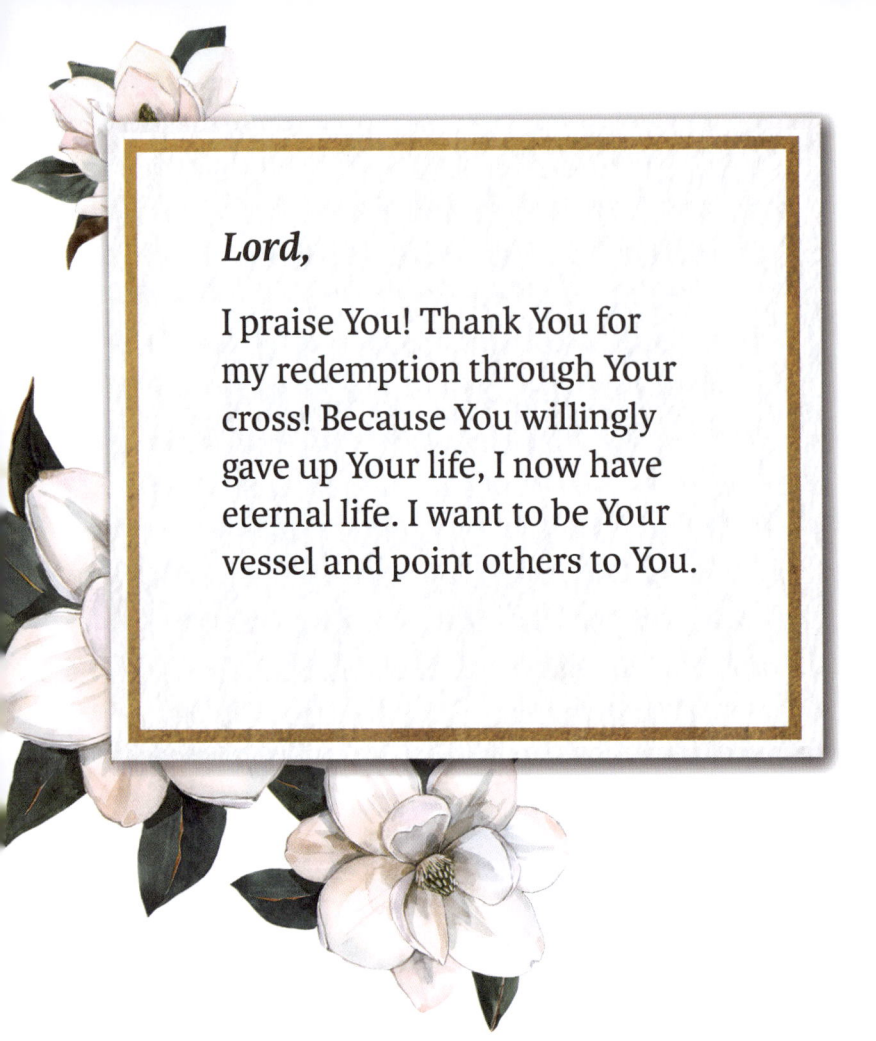

I praise You! Thank You for my redemption through Your cross! Because You willingly gave up Your life, I now have eternal life. I want to be Your vessel and point others to You.

For there is one God, and one mediator also between God and men, the man Christ Jesus, who gave Himself as a ransom for all.

1 TIMOTHY 2:5-6a

Lord God,

I am in awe of You. I think about Your creation, the magnificence of Your work, and yet how personally accessible You are to me. You desire for me to spend time with You. I'm amazed, Lord, even speechless.

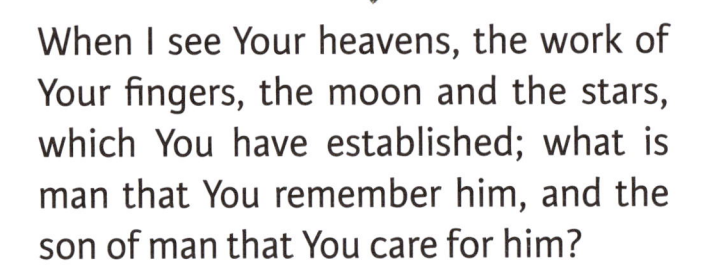

When I see Your heavens, the work of Your fingers, the moon and the stars, which You have established; what is man that You remember him, and the son of man that You care for him?

PSALM 8:3-4

My Lord,

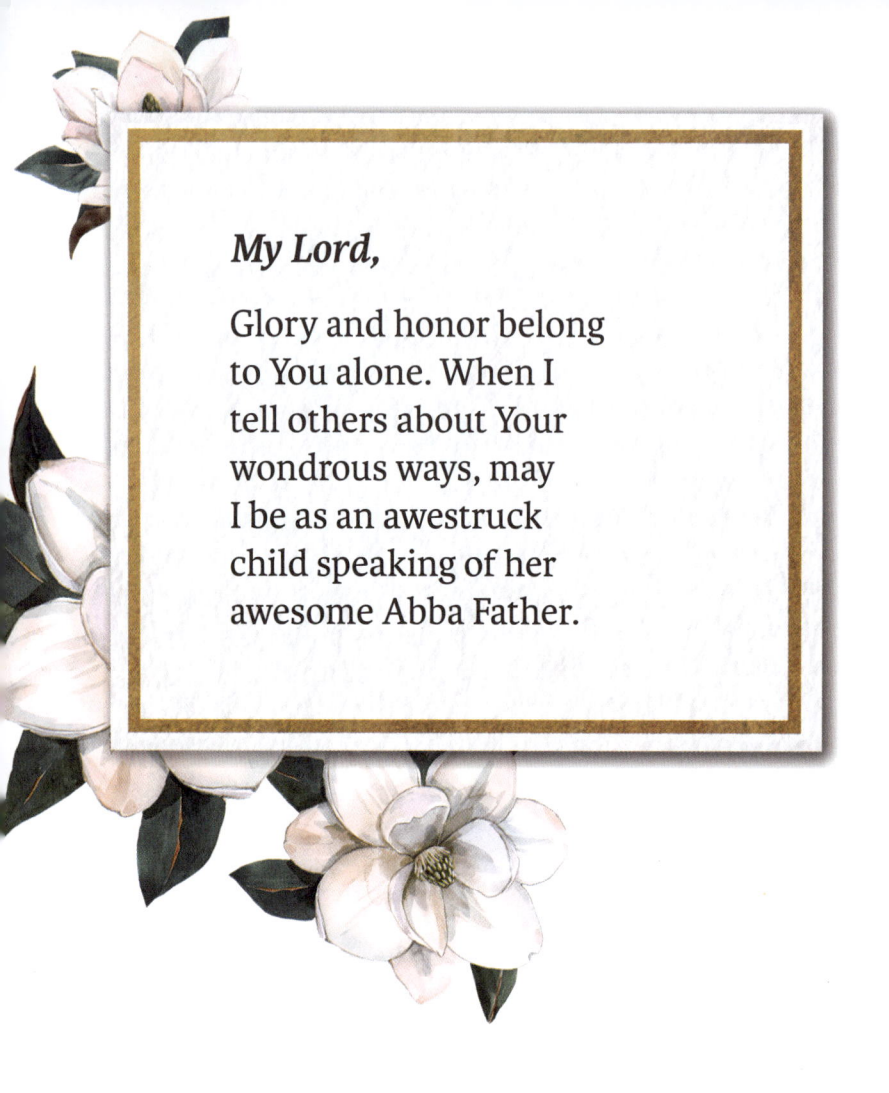

Glory and honor belong to You alone. When I tell others about Your wondrous ways, may I be as an awestruck child speaking of her awesome Abba Father.

And because you are sons, God sent forth the Spirit of His Son into our hearts, crying, "Abba! Father!"

GALATIANS 4:6

Jesus,

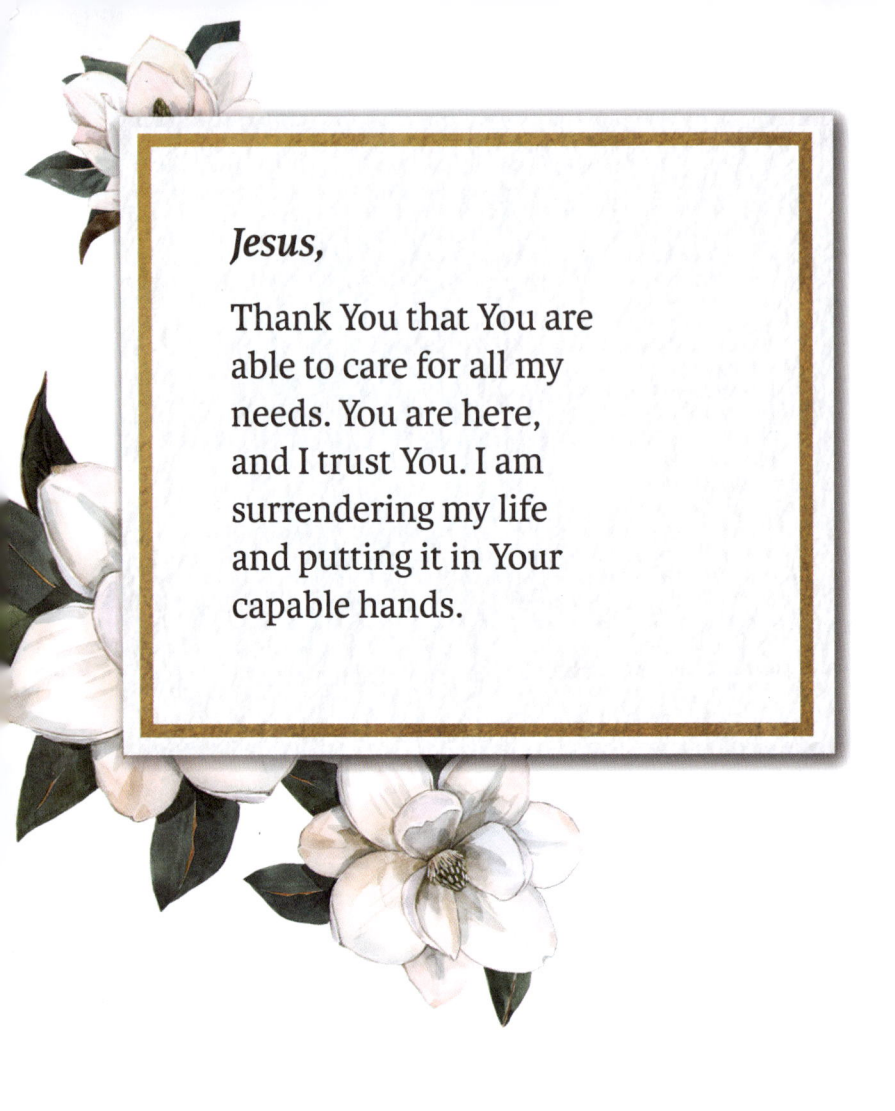

Thank You that You are able to care for all my needs. You are here, and I trust You. I am surrendering my life and putting it in Your capable hands.

And He is before all things,
and in Him all things hold together.

COLOSSIANS 1:17

Lord,

There are times You seem distant. I know my feelings and emotions can cloud the truth. Anchor me to Your Word today. Stir my mind to the Scriptures that You have planted in my heart. You are the rock of my salvation. May I hold fast to You whenever life's storms bellow.

Therefore we do not lose heart, but though our outer man is decaying, yet our inner man is being renewed day by day. For our momentary, light affliction is working out for us an eternal weight of glory far beyond all comparison.

2 CORINTHIANS 4:16-17

Lord,

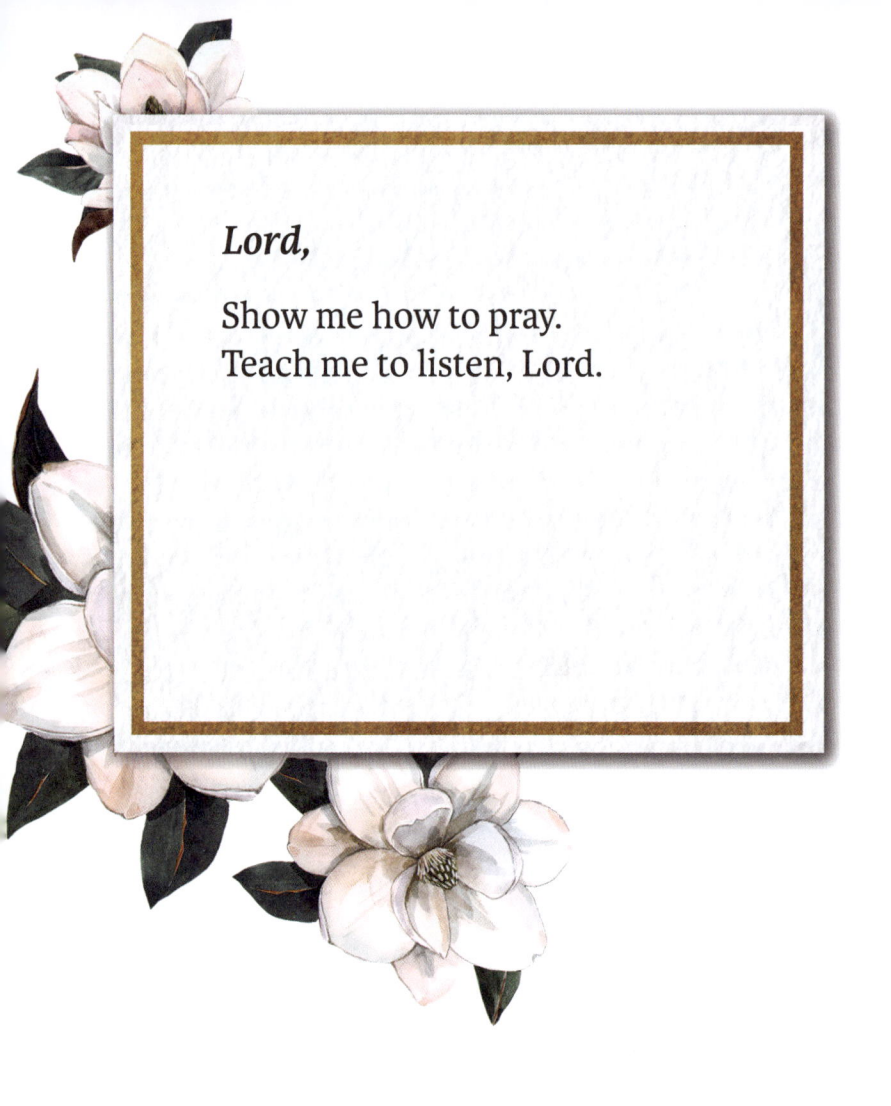

Show me how to pray.
Teach me to listen, Lord.

Cease striving and know that I am God.

PSALM 46:10a

Jesus,

It's because of Your blood that I am washed clean. Through Your victory I am set free from guilt and shame. Help me to move forward in the newness of life that You have given me.

Therefore, brothers, since we have confidence to enter the holy places by the blood of Jesus, let us draw near with a sincere heart in full assurance of faith, having our hearts sprinkled from an evil conscience and our bodies washed with pure water.

HEBREWS 10:19, 22